Dear Deb!
Be blessed!
Be inspired!
Be hopeful!
Much love
Gayle
Suzanne

It's In The Little Things

An inspirational and humorous book about
living a life of happiness and abundance.

Gayle Suzanne

It's In The Little Things

An inspirational and humorous book about living a life of happiness and abundance.

Gayle Suzanne

Charlton, MA 01507

Visit my website at www.gaylesuzanne.com

Email me at gayle@gaylesuzanne.com

Dedication

This book is dedicated to my niece, Heather and daughter, Becca.

Heather has given me so much courage and inspiration! She has no idea how much her support and confidence has helped me reach my goals and achieve my dreams. Sometimes it takes a special person to see what you cannot see for yourself.

Becca has truly made me see what beauty means inside and out. She has taught me so much about myself. My motivation to become healthier really kicked into gear after she was born. It was so important for me to be a positive, loving role model to her. She is my most precious gift and I'm so proud of the confident, self-assured, beautiful person she is today.

Table of Contents

Preface

Our lives can be inundated with trials and pain. Somewhere in between our struggles we might lose hope for living a fulfilling, enjoyable life.

The first part of my life was filled with challenges: emotional abuse, a mother who struggled with alcohol, bullying, low self-esteem, sexual abuse and countless rejections. During most of my early years I had a nagging feeling that I was damaged and not good enough. I dreamed of a life where I felt happy but became resolved in thinking that a great life was meant for others but not for me.

Today I have a wonderful life. It is not without its problems, but I have learned to look at life through a different lens.

This book is about loving God, loving yourself and loving others. I believe that through the little things you can find the fulfillment and happiness you desire. With storytelling and personal experiences, I share ideas and lessons that have had the most transforming impact on my life. Some are lighthearted and others are more emotional and deep. Most have messages of how to appreciate seemingly insignificant events and how to take minor steps to improve your circumstances. If you commit to take action and look at things differently, you will see yourself and those around you change. My intent is not to hurt anyone, but to tell my truth.

I pressed through difficult situations coming out on the other side living a blessed life I am truly grateful for.

Obstacles can bring us down but after we dust off and pick ourselves up, those obstacles can be valuable lessons in disguise. Through the ups and downs of life, we become transformed into the strong, beautiful people we are today.

PART 1

Bullying and Unkindness

Gayle Suzanne

Treat Others As You Would Like To Be Treated, *Regardless*

Many of us learned this golden rule at a young age. Our parents and teachers would tell us not to say something nasty to someone we would not like if they said the same thing to us. Make sure you treat other people the way you want to be treated yourself.

It makes sense. If someone is nice to you, the right and relatively easy thing to do is be nice to them back. We all pretty much get that. If someone invites me to dinner, the right thing for me to do is to reciprocate and invite her to dinner. Life works beautifully when it is a back and forth thing.

Well, what happens when someone does not get you a gift and you got them one? What happens when someone is rude to you in a store? What happens when you let someone go ahead of you in traffic and they do not wave to thank you? What happens when someone cuts you off and grabs the parking space you have been waiting five minutes for with your blinker on in the rain? What happens when you love someone and they do not love you back?

Years ago when I was hospitalized for an intestinal issue, I was having a horrible bout of nausea. I had been vomiting non-stop for about twenty minutes and my call button fell on the floor. My hospital roommate was out of the room so I could not ask her to push her button. My bed was closest to the door and I called out to a woman who was walking down the hallway. I said excuse me and asked her to please call a nurse for me. The woman was stunning with long golden, blonde hair and wore a striking pink suit. She was carrying a clip board so I assumed she was a hospital employee. She looked at me without entering the room. I asked again for help. She asked, "Can't you call someone yourself?" In between gags I told her my button had fallen on the floor. Now granted, I was gagging and vomiting so I did not expect her to come into the room, pick up my button and clean my face, but I would have appreciated her telling a nurse I was sick. Another fifteen minutes or so went by and no one came. My roommate returned from her tests and immediately pushed her button for me. My nurse came, gave me some drugs and I was happy.

An hour or so later, the woman in pink returned. This time she entered the room, walked right past me and said hello to my roommate.

She said, "Hi. I'm Beth. I am a minister and I'm here to pray for you."

The most valuable lessons come in the strangest ways. As I think about this incident and if I take my own advice, if I ever see this woman again and she needs help, I would have to help her.

This is probably one of the hardest challenges in life. Be kind. Ignore bad behavior when you can. Confront if you must, but be calm and always approach someone with respect. It is quite a challenge.

Sticks And Stones... Bla Bla Bla

Sticks and stones can break my bones but words will never hurt me. We've all heard it before.

I don't buy it. *Sometimes* we have the strength within not to allow hurtful words to affect us. Many times we don't.

I will never forget an incident that completely changed my outlook on the impact of words. I was walking down the street in a nearby small town. Two women, who looked to be in their twenties, were walking in front of me with a small boy, no more than three years old. He was absolutely adorable dressed in little blue jeans and a denim jacket. The women were moving at a swift pace and the little boy was having a hard time keeping up. Other than thinking he was cute, I didn't pay too much attention to them at first. Then he tripped and fell on the concrete sidewalk. The woman (I can only assume was his mother) told him to get up. Her exact words: *"Get up you fucking little asshole. I can't believe what a klutz you are. Clumsy ass."*

My face dropped. I literally stood still, paralyzed. After he got up, they walked around the corner and disappeared. It took a minute for my shock to dissipate. As I write this, some thirty years later, I regret not running over to him, scooping him up and telling him he is a precious, special little boy. Instead, I did nothing but listen in horror. Until that moment I was not fully aware of how powerful words can be.

You may remember someone saying something hurtful to you that has been seared into your heart. I know I have.

Negative words can make a lasting, if not lifelong, impact. In my younger years, people said vicious things about me that have scarred me. I believed those statements were truth. Those statements impacted my life to the point where I was convinced I was damaged and defective. Negative words can certainly alter one's path, set limiting beliefs, and hold someone back from accomplishing the great things they were meant to accomplish. If someone hears he is not smart enough, he might believe that statement his entire life. If he hears he is not good enough, he might hold on to that thought his entire life.

What I know now is that unkind statements made by others are not necessarily truth.

As an adult I had to relearn my truth. Just because my name unfortunately rhymed with a nasty word, it did not mean I **was** that nasty word.

I had to relearn that I am a valuable person who is worthy of love regardless of what spewed out of someone's mouth. I had to understand that if someone said something intentionally to hurt me, it did not mean they were right. It could have meant that they were lashing out because someone hurt them and that's all they knew.

As I matured I made a conscious decision to surround myself with people who would lift me up and encourage me and not tear me down. With the help of loving family and friends and deep soul searching, I realized that sometimes people say cruel things when they are hurting, and those words have nothing to do with me.

Years ago I learned a simple technique which helped me protect myself from unkind words. If someone said something mean, I would visualize a thick plastic shield covering my chest. To me, the shield would protect my heart and it would repel anything negative. The shield stops painful untruths from entering my being.

From time to time I think of that little boy when I see bullying on TV or on a playground. He taught me that I should take every opportunity I can to say positive, uplifting, and encouraging words to others. We should lift each other up. So when you get aggravated or upset, take a couple of breaths before you say something hurtful to someone else, because cruel words have the potential to hurt and scar for life.

I'll make up my own saying: *Sticks and stones can break my bones, but hurtful words will never come out of my mouth.*

Gayle Suzanne

Heavy

I've had a weight problem for as long as I can remember. I was a bit chubby as a child. I have pictures of me in a blue and white polka-dot bikini when I was about two years old. If I had not been female, I could have easily been mistaken for a mini Buddha. I always wore a goofy hat (a tradition I passed on to my daughter) and posed with my belly sticking straight out. As I got older I grew taller and my physique was average. A little chub here and there, but noting out of the ordinary.

When I was just shy of my twelfth birthday, I had my first kiss. I had dreamed of this kiss for so long-- watching people eat other people's faces on TV was so intriguing to me. How does she know where to put her nose? What does it feel like? What if the boy I had a crush on in English class wants to kiss me in the hallway after school? Or in the moonlight after tennis practice? As a young girl entering puberty, I could spend hours wrapped up in those thoughts.

But it turned that out my first kiss was not the fantasy smooch I had dreamed of from one of my cute classmates or neighbors. It was from a man in his forties. This was not a man who coerced me into his car to pet his puppy. He did not offer me candy at the park. I was not afraid of him. He was not a creep. He was someone I knew and trusted.

Without revealing too much detail, once his body pressed up against mine forcefully, I went numb thinking that there is no way this is happening. I believe my mind left my body for a short period of time. After my senses returned, I realized I was being pushed up against a wall by his much larger frame. As a young girl without any formal wrestling training, I was unsure how to maneuver myself out of this unnatural predicament. But somewhere, somehow, the strength of Popeye after eating his spinach burst out of me. I was able to push him off and run away to safety. You know that story when someone lifts a car to rescue someone? That is the only way I can describe my strength in that moment. I believe it was a divine intervention.

I was physically free from him, but not without emotional scarring. Not long afterwards, I believe I unconsciously developed a protective mechanism to prevent an incident like that from ever happening again. I began to eat more comfort foods-- anything sweet-- cookies, cakes, brownies. I gained quite a bit of weight. As a pre-teen who did not tell a soul what happened, I had to find a way, on my own, to protect myself. Sweets provided me comfort. Part of me felt shame, that I had somehow provoked his actions. By standing near him talking about my English test, did I somehow encourage his advances? It took me years to believe I did absolutely nothing wrong. There were multitudes of emotional issues I had to come to grips with. Things I did not understand. I dealt with them silently. The only way I knew to ease the pain was to fill myself up with food to take away the disbelief, pain and shame.

As I started to gain weight, I felt secure that older men would not find me appealing and therefore would not make sexual advances toward me. That was a very good thing. I believed I created the boundary I needed to keep them away, so there would never be a repeat incident.

But at the same time, what I really wanted was for a boy my age to like me. To love me. To show me that I was worthy of being loved. I wanted to experience a romantic kiss with a sixth grader! I was at that tender pre-teen age when boys started asking girls out. I did acknowledge to myself that if I gained weight the boys my age would *not* find me appealing. I also knew that my weight was one of the reasons I was being taunted at school. On one hand I wanted to be invisible to any man over forty, on the other hand, I wanted to be loved. I must have subconsciously made the decision that being heavy was the path I had to take, because I knew I could never endure another incident like that again. This unconscious thought was a protective mechanism for me (You can tell I went to counseling). I knew I was sabotaging what I really wanted, but on the flip side, I was safe. What a catch-22.

Over the years I have lost, gained, lost, gained, lost, gained. My name should be yo-yo. This back and forth weight gain is something that I am finally ready to deal with now that I am approaching the golden years. I have come to a place of peace where most of the time I am able to accept me as I am (squishy parts and all), but I think it is time to grow (mentally, not physically) and relearn how to nourish myself properly.

So when you see someone who is heavy, there might be a bit more to their story than you realize. Be kind to others. You really never know what they have gone through and how they got to where they are.

By the way, took me years and years and years and years, but I have forgiven him.

Bullying

I think it is important to write the truth and the feelings that go along with what bullying did to me.

As a child I was sensitive and insecure. Even though I did well in school, played the organ and won awards, loved animals, was funny and had a big heart, as a young girl I believed I was not worth much. I was naïve and gullible in social situations. I was overly trustworthy and my heart broke easily. I was rejected time and again but tried to make friends. I had a few that I would cling to. I had sleepovers with these few friends and we would dance in my room and sing into the hairbrush. We would fantasize about being married to our favorite teen heartthrob. One of my school friends, Kim, used to visit, but my dog Mike would hump her every time he saw her so eventually she stopped coming over.

My first negative experience with a close friend was with my neighbor, Anna, who moved from another state to live with her dad. At first, our friendship was awesome. We would blast single records on her stereo. We played Barbies, board games, rode bikes and drew pictures. Eventually we started hanging out with another neighbor Darcy, who was one year older than me. The three of us were best buds. I was seven years old and in second grade at the time. One day when we were in Anna's room dancing and singing, Anna started taking off her clothes. She wanted to show us a striptease. I remember feeling uncomfortable, but curious. She was not developed and had the same stuff as I did. I knew it was wrong to watch her but I did not leave or say anything. After several weekends of watching her strip during our dance time (it became a frequent event), Anna asked Darcy and me to take our clothes off. I did not want to. Instinctively I knew it was wrong. Darcy did not want to either but she removed her clothes anyway. She was a year older and more developed. My gut told me it was wrong so I said no and kept my clothes on. I wanted to keep my private parts to myself.

That was the start of it. Anna was quite upset with me for not stripping and she started calling me names. Darcy was much nicer but was more of a follower so she followed suit. I left soon after the dance show was over. I knew this was not going to be good.

I began to feel out of place when we hung out but still wanted to play with them. We lived on a pond and Anna had a tire rope swing. In the summer we would swing on the tire and jump off into the pond. During a cold winter day someone had the grand idea of swinging on the tire. There was snow on the ground and there was a light coat of ice on the pond, but not thick enough to hold anyone. We put our hooded parkas on and headed toward the swing. Both girls got on before me and swung back and forth over the partially frozen pond. When it was my turn I jumped on the tire and immediately they gave me a big push. My balance must have been off because I slid off the tire in an instant. It only took a few seconds before I broke through the ice and was submerged in the freezing cold water. All I remember was laughter! LOUD laughter. I started to cry and pulled myself up onto the sandy beach area. I was drenched, humiliated, embarrassed, crushed and utterly ashamed. They were laughing, calling me "Baby! Baby! Baby!" I ran home completely soaked and crying. I never hung out with those girls after that.

I was hurt by the situation but it was not the end of my world. It was uncomfortable when I saw them but they were the first girls that actually made fun of me. I could make other friends. I knew I could. But somehow the teasing went beyond the neighborhood and started at the bus stop. Many mornings waiting for the bus I would stand with a couple of tougher neighborhood kids. They would make comments and make fun of me on most days. I remember wishing I was invisible. I thought if I was invisible then they would have nothing to say because I did not exist. How can you make fun of something that is not there?

One day I was getting off the bus and was wearing a hat with a tie underneath my chin. I usually walked home in the opposite direction of one of the meaner girls. This day she decided to follow me. She jumped up on my back and tried to yank the hat off of my head. She could not pull it off because it was tied to my chin. The yarn stretched tight around my neck and it was choking me. She was just laughing while she was hanging on my back pulling harder. This particular day my mother and sister protectors came down to the bus stop and witnessed what was happening. My mother yelled at her to get off of me. Thanks Ma and Chris - right time right place - whew! The mean girl jumped off me and went home. I was so grateful they were there at that moment. They saved me...and my hat!

My reaction to this incident: first disbelief, then shame. I never fought back, never spoke up for myself. I just took it. Way down deep inside I thought I deserved it. I must be different or weird or just plain unlovable and this is why people treated me the way they did.

In sixth grade I became friends with a popular girl. We talked at every recess and went to dances together. I became close friends with some of her friends. They were all pretty, smart and popular and knew a lot of boys. For that year I felt good and believed things were turning around for the better. I had a great summer with my new friends and was invited to parties and sleepovers.

Then next year we entered Junior High. For some reason, early on in the year, my popular friend turned on me. Her friends turned on me. This was such a quick transition from being her best friend one day to being the object of her hatred the next. The malice she felt for me was undeniable. As I look back I realized I always sought her approval. I became insecure and paranoid. I asked frequently if she was mad at me. She was not honest with me. The distance between us made me feel that I did something wrong. I wanted to have an open communication but the more I wanted that, the more she pulled away.

It started off that she and her friends would not speak to me. These girls were the people I spent most of my time with so I instantly blamed myself (for what I don't know) and it hurt me so much. I did not know what I had done and felt like a target. During class I would hear whispers about how fat, gross, disgusting or stupid I was. During gym, standing there in my polyester one-piece maroon striped gym suit (remember those?) I was picked last. Somehow "my friend" managed to get most of the other kids in the class to think I was a loser. They either would not acknowledge me or made fun of me. This went on for the entire seventh and eighth grade years. I went to a dance and a boy asked me to dance. When I said yes (and felt so happy inside!) he said, "Why would I dance with someone like *you!* Ha Ha Ha!" I think Stephen King's movie "Carrie" was playing in the movie theaters at this time and boy could I relate to her! Except for the pig's blood-- no one ever dumped a bucket of pig's blood on my head-- thank goodness! For almost two years I was made fun of daily and I hated the person I was. I felt alone and unlovable. I felt defective.

I was fortunate to have two friends throughout this time. They were twin sisters who lived a few streets away from me. They were nice, smart and kind. They were not mean girls and I somehow managed to keep them as friends during this time. I found safety and acceptance in their company. Talk about a double blessing!

It makes me sad remembering a specific memory of eighth grade. To get to my class I had to walk by this huge mirrored showcase with our schools trophies in it. One morning I was going to one of my classes and someone had just made a "funny" derogatory remark about me. I felt close to tears (although I never *ever* cried in front of these mean kids. Good for me!). As I walked past that mirror I saw my face. I actually saw so much fear in my eyes it almost stopped me in my tracks. My facial expression revealed absolute terror. Part of me felt bad for myself and the other part thought, "Wow, Gayle, if you look that scared no wonder people zeroed in on you!"

The repeated harassment of others took its toll on me. I had suicidal thoughts during the end of my eighth grade year. I remember faking a sore throat and stayed home from school for over a week. I was at the end of my rope and could not take the daily pressure anymore. I did not have it in me to go back to school again. I was never physically hurt by these kids, but the emotional abuse I endured was damaging. It damaged me at my core. I had so much shame. The shame consumed me. I was ashamed that I was one of "those" kids and ashamed that I was not liked.

My family did know some of what I was going through and they felt terrible. At the end of my eighth grade year, my parents set up an interview for me at a nearby private high school. This was one of the best things they ever did for me. I passed the admission test and started my freshman year with a clean slate. That was the beginning of a new life for me where I met true lifetime friends.

I am thankful that bullying awareness has been heightened in recent years. I am passionate about this topic and fully understand its impact. I hope young people begin to realize the effect of constant bullying. I also hope the ones that have been bullied realize that they are special and loveable just the way they are, regardless what anyone says.

And just a quick note to all those who were mean to me, "Look at me now!"

The "Cool" Crowd

It is interesting to think about the whole concept of the "cool kids." The ones I grew up with picked on and humiliated some of the nicest kids I knew. Marie was picked on all through Junior High also. She was sweet, smart, kind, silly, and interesting. Her parents were strict and she was sheltered and shy. She minded her own business every day on the bus and during school, yet she was tortured every day. Some days watching her being tortured by other kids took the focus away from me and I felt relief because at least one person was picked on more than me. I always felt guilty about that, but she was my wall of safety. I remember one day we were on the bus on the way home from school and her stop was the street before mine. She was in front of me waiting to get off and the bus stopped short. She lost her footing and fell down the steps and her butt was stuck in between the door and the first step. Everyone behind me on the bus roared with laughter. That happened forty years ago and I still remember her face-- the embarrassment, the shame, the humiliation. I still remember the vicious laughter surrounding her.

I've thought about that incident many times over the years. That fall could have happened to anyone standing in that spot. The cheerleader, the football quarterback, the pot head, the pageant queen. It was so unfortunate that it happened to Marie. I think of people that have been picked on and their lives may have been molded by the abuse they suffered. The image I had of myself was molded by others. I felt worthless, damaged and no good.

In more recent times, I recall an occasion when I was at a school sporting event. I was sitting alone on the field. Down the field there was a group of five women who usually sat together and always seemed like they were having a good time. I usually sat by myself or with another friend, yet I would say hi to the group of women as I walked by. This particular day my friend was not at the game so I sat near the other women and initiated a conversation. I tried to make small talk for a few minutes but did not get a warm response. I honestly felt like I was back in Junior High School. Their coolness implied that I was not good enough to be in their company. I was forty-one-years-old. I thought it was ridiculous. I felt slightly rejected and a small pang of hurt rushed through my body. I stayed where I was and did not continue in conversation. I sat quietly and watched the game. Then one of the mothers started saying negative comments about one of the kids on the field. As she rolled her eyes, she said in a rude and disgusted manner that the young girl was not running fast enough and should not be playing that position at all.

It took everything in my power not to say anything to her. I knew if I did it would not have done any good. After my initial irritation of hearing this mother talk trash about another child on the team, I picked up my chair and moved to the other side of the field. I thought about what just happened. My motive for going over there in the first place was to get in with the cool crowd. I had that yearning to be right in there with them, to be accepted and to feel cool. When I was snubbed, my instant reaction was that I was not good enough to socialize with them. As I sat with that thought for a minute, I had to tell myself that no one is better than me. It had nothing to do with me. It had to do with them. They were rude and unfriendly and went out of their way to make me feel unwelcome. Then they went out of their way to gossip about a young kid who was trying her best on the field. The thought of those comments coming out of my mouth was absurd, because it never would happen.

Who is one person to say that another is not good enough? We all are special and wonderful in our own ways. I basically was a shy kid who was not strong enough to fight for myself. I was sensitive, smart, good hearted, kind, funny, quick-witted, humble, and honest. These are not qualities of a loser; quite the contrary. People are targeted for bullying for whatever reason, but most people who are bullied are wonderful people. They are just a target.

I only wish I knew as a kid what I know now. There was nothing wrong with me or Marie or anyone else. Period. *Nothing wrong with us!* The feelings of humiliation are bigger than life but you have to hold onto the thought that every one of us is God's child. I kept on hearing that God does not make junk. Marie was not junk, and I was not junk either. Even though others picked on me and thought I was a loser, it was just their opinion. And they were wrong.

I made up my mind later on in life that I would really work on myself and try not to allow another person to make me feel bad about myself. I would still be accountable for my actions and take responsibility for my wrong doings when I hurt someone, but I was not going to allow anyone to make me feel less than a whole person. Everyone has faults, no one is perfect. If someone has more money than I do, they are not better. If someone has a more beautiful face, they are not better. If someone can talk in front of a crowd with ease, they are not better. If someone has a twenty inch waist, they are not better. If someone has more musical talent, they are not better. If someone thinks they're better, that does not make it so. We all have different qualities; we are all unique and fabulously wonderful in our own way.

PART 2

Developing a Healthy Self

Gayle Suzanne

Let It Go

If you think about an incident that happened thirteen years ago on May 10th at 5:47pm and your heart still races, your back still stiffens up and you take your anger out on those around you, it might be time to let it go.

If you do not let things go, you might experience some of the following physical symptoms:

- migraines

- breaking out

- forehead veins popping out

- crabbiness and irritability

- sweaty palms

- high blood pressure

- rapid heart beat

- upset stomach

- clenched teeth

- tight fists

- squeaky loud voice

- red tomato face

- gagging

- shaking

I often thought that letting go meant I was letting the other person off the hook for hurting me. If I let it go, I believed I was saying it was perfectly okay that they did what they did. I actually thought that holding on to my anger made me a stronger person. I believed it was weakness on my part to let it go.

Meanwhile, while I am aggravated thinking of every tiny detail of the incident, all this unpleasant, unhealthy stuff is happening to my body. Simultaneously, the person I am upset with is casually eating a bologna sandwich-- not an ounce of thought coming my way.

I guess this explains why letting go is a favor you do for *yourself,* not for the other person. For peace of mind, mental health and living a positive lifestyle, it is in my best interest to let it go. How on earth is raising my blood pressure "getting back" at the other person?

I did not say it was easy, but it is something beneficial you can do for yourself. When something happens and you become upset, **feel it.** Feel the hurt, the anger, the sadness, the disappointment, and the frustration. Do what you have to do: punch a pillow, vent to a friend, run down the street screaming (make sure you watch out for cars), get on the elliptical machine, take a long soothing bath, have a gut-wrenching cry, listen to loud music. Do whatever works for you. Sometimes writing your honest thoughts in a journal can help. Try anything in a *balanced, healthy* way to release your frustration. Feel what you need to feel until it is out of your system. If you find yourself getting irritated about the same thing again, take a deep breath and release it. Release until you do not give it a second thought.

Stuff happens in life and it is for *your own benefit* to let it go. Just think how much money you'll save on that mouth guard!

Gayle Suzanne

Concentrate On Your Gift And Talents

We have different gifts, according to the grace given to us. If a man's gift is prophesying, let him use it in proportion to his faith. If it is serving, let him serve; it if is teaching, let him teach; if it is encouraging, let him encourage; if it contributing to the needs of others, let him give generously, if it is leadership, let him govern diligently; if it is showing mercy, let him do it cheerfully.

Romans 12:6

We can be so hard on ourselves. We get discouraged because we cannot make it through spin class, cook a gourmet meal or understand a complicated spreadsheet.

"My house isn't as nicely decorated as my neighbor's."

"I can't sew my own curtains like my mother did."

"I stink at baseball. All the other players are better than me."

"My cucumbers are tiny compared to my neighbors. I'm a failure!"

For years I have berated myself because of things I could not do or did not excel at. I fully realize there are many things I cannot do, but I have learned to strengthen and build upon the things I *can* do.

We compare, we see things that others accomplish and we want the same thing. We tend to focus on the things that we cannot do. Yep, sometimes we even obsess over them.

Imagine that! I will be happy when I can do this. I will be happy when I can do that. The thing is we all have talents and gifts that are unique to us as individuals.

The feeling of "I can't do this well" or "I don't get it" had become too overwhelming for me. I wanted to be content the way I was and accept me for me. I also yearned to discover hidden talents that might be tucked away somewhere. I was determined to find out exactly what they were. So I ventured out and took a bite out of life. We all have our own special gifts but it is completely up to us to unearth our own talents.

I attended wine tasting events, even though as a general rule, I throw up after drinking wine. I signed up for pottery class but each time I tried to mold a vase it looked just like a penis. No wonder no one ever ate candy out of there! I went to a bartending class but realized I would rather drink than pour. I worked out at the gym but was totally uncomfortable when toned, thin people effortlessly tread-milled next to me.

I thought I might do well in accounting so I signed up for an intro class in college. Five months into the semester, we were in class reviewing for the final exam. My professor wrote some complicated equation on the board and asked the class, "What is this?" I turned to my super smart friend and said, "This is accounting, isn't it?" I received an 11 on that final (an 11 out of 100, not 12).

I also tried a few political science courses and realized I loved them! I went on to a thirty-year relatively satisfying legal career. So I never became partner in an accounting firm, but I was a pretty darn talented paralegal.

My daughter, Becca, loves math-- a trait that was most definitely not passed down from me. She is a math major in college and wants to teach high school. I asked her what kind of math she wants to teach. She replied, "Well, Algebra relaxes me. It calms me to figure out a problem. But Statistics-- that EXCITES me! I get excited trying to figure it out!!" I glanced at her like she just grew another head.

My friend's first job was a waitress in a seafood restaurant. On her first shift, a customer ordered a lobster dinner. She took the order perfectly and placed it in front of him. "Would you like anything else, sir?" He asked for crackers. She returned with a package of Saltines. Needless to say, her career in waitressing was not meant to be. She went on to be an incredible special needs teacher.

To aid in discovering my individual gifts, I signed up for anything that piqued my interest. If you do not know what you have a passion for, get out there and find out! Join a pool league, sign up for charity walks, strip wallpaper and renovate a house for a children's charity, serve dinner at an elderly function, take ceramics, learn how to change the oil in your car, sell homemade crafts at a fair, try Bikram yoga, adopt a pet, paint a picture, lead a group, go for a hike in the mountains. The list goes on forever. Somewhere in there you will unveil your true passion.

Gayle Suzanne

The Church In Canada

Fear was a dominant emotion throughout my younger years. I was afraid of everything. As a child, my reaction to fear usually resulted in panic and hysterical crying. When I became frightened, I would seek out my older sister, Chris, for protection. She is three years older than me and was definitely the wiser and calmer sibling growing up. I looked up to her and relied on her to guide me through any situation. At night, I would attempt to sleep in my own bed but eventually ended up sleeping in her bed. I felt safe next to her.

One bizarre incident stands out in my mind to demonstrate the intensity of my fear as a young girl. I have quite a bit of emotion attached to this story but wanted to share it to demonstrate the impact of fear and how one can overcome and move forward.

When I was nine years old my family took a vacation to Canada. On our list of stops was a cathedral. My mother loved old churches and museums. She enjoyed each painting and sculpture so much that she would stare at them for at least twenty minutes each (as a young child, it felt like an eternity). Her appreciation of art was intense but for nine-year-old me, it was torturous boredom.

We visited this cathedral during the winter and we were *finally* leaving. Outside there was snow and frozen icy patches on the ground. I noticed the parking lot appeared circular and thought I would run off to the left, circle around the lot and meet everyone at the car. I needed to burn off some energy after being cooped inside for hours.

As I was running I realized that I had gone to a lower lot. Our car was in the upper lot. In between the lots was a huge rock cliff wall covered in snow and ice. I noticed that the parking lot was not circular like I had thought. It just went downhill. Further below I did not see a curve to loop around to get to our car. My parents and sister had gone the direct route so they were probably at the car by now.

From where I stood, I heard a car start in the upper lot. In that instant, *insane* fear and panic set it. I can honestly say this fear was tremendous. It was sheer panic. I could not breathe. I swore it was my car that had started and my family was getting ready to leave me in Canada.

I immediately thought I had to get to them the quickest way possible so they would see me before they left for the next stop. I could backtrack and run back to where we all started together outside the cathedral and find the car the way we came in or I could go the more direct route and climb the cliff. I heard the car start somewhere above me, so I thought the car was just over the rocky cliff. I started to climb. I had on a winter coat but was not wearing gloves or a hat. The cliff appeared to be a story or two high. It looked huge to me. As I started to climb I had to grab onto rocks that were covered with ice and snow. My hands and fingers were bleeding from the sharp ice which covered the rocks. I was hysterical as I continued to climb. I kept praying that they would not leave me there. The only thing I concentrated on was the sound of the car humming somewhere above me.

I finally made it to the top and looked around frantically and saw that my family was standing outside the car looking in all directions. I ran over to them with frozen tears stuck to my face. I was so relieved to see them. They hugged me yet could not believe I thought they would *actually leave me in Canada.*

I had to go back into the cathedral and clean myself off. I was whimpering and really holding back my wailing. My chin quivered but I knew I was safe now. I was so relieved that I was not going to be an orphan in Canada. I liked Massachusetts.

I had to do some serious work to diminish my fears. Trusting God, letting go and counseling changed the way I live my life. Fear has probably been the most challenging obstacle for me to face. I was open to anything that could take it away and for me, trusting in God and letting fear go was the only way I could release it. Today, I do not live in constant fear and I am so grateful. Just goes to show that if you work and pray on an issue, over time you very well might be freed from its chains.

The God Box

Yep, I have one. Sometimes it takes me a while to get it out and put stuff in it, but I definitely have one. The God box could be a special box with crystal baubles on it, could be a wooden cedar chest, could be a drawer in your jewelry box, could be a shoebox or could be a leftover Chinese food takeout container. It does not matter what kind of box it is. The God box is just a symbol to help you let go and let God.

God grant me the serenity to accept the things I cannot change, the courage to change the things I can, and the wisdom to know the difference.

That prayer is so beautiful and simple, yet it is so difficult to live by. I know though, when I do abide by that prayer that all things work out for good. The reason it is difficult for me is that when something is aggravating me or I am fearful about something, I try everything in my own power to solve the situation myself. My will, my way, what I want, the way I want it. I go through a million different ways to change the situation to suit my needs and what I think is in my best interest. After all of my efforts, when nothing happens, or worse, when something happens that is not in my plan, I get irritated and frustrated.

Let's use a simple example. If my husband does not like cabbage and I want him to like cabbage, no amount of nagging, manipulating, coercing, griping, complaining, or conniving is going to make him like cabbage. If I am trying to change someone and they do not want to change, that is something I have to accept.

So when I get irritated, rather than trying to do something about something I cannot change, I need to write down what is upsetting me and put it in the God box! When I place it in the God box, to me, that means God is handling the problem now - whatever it is. Now I can go about my life in a peaceful and content manner. It is a wonderful feeling to be able to let the situation go and let God solve it in His time. The main problem for me is that I keep going back in the box and try another solution. Then I put it back in the God box when that solution does not work.

It is a process, but once you put something in the God box and really surrender and let it go, miraculous things happen. I have put my fears in the God box over and over and over and over again, and over time they have diminished greatly. This tool is a wonderful symbolization of letting go and letting God.

Who Cares If You Look Like A Monkey?

My mid-thirties was a time to rediscover life. I sought opportunities to experiment with new adventures. One place I had heard about was a yoga facility that offered a variety of interesting workshops. I booked a weekend and off I went.

I arrived at the Kripalu center mid-morning on a Friday. My curiosity intensified as I anticipated this foreign adventure! Little did I know it was the beginning of doing a whole slew of things on my own. I might as well start enjoying me.

I parked and walked through the front door. I wore a pair of white capris, fashionable white flat sandals and a pink shirt with little sequins on it. When I opened the door and took my first peek inside, I was greeted by men dressed in ponchos and clogs and women with hairy legs. No one was wearing cute little sandals or glitz of any kind. Luckily I had packed some casual workout clothes so I was able to comfortably blend in. The center was huge with a long hallway of rooms. It had previously been a monastery and was stark but peaceful. My room was simple with a twin bed, sink and a dresser. I changed into sweats, wiped off my makeup, tied up my sneakers, packed away my large hoop earings, closed the door and prepared to explore.

I felt safe here. I had a feeling I was going to heal a part of myself this weekend. There was a sense of acceptance and belonging. I was ready to move forward with my life as a self-assured, confident woman, but I had to learn to accept and embrace all of me. I knew I was in the right place.

There was an African Dance class just beginning. The room was packed and I was intrigued. The loud drum banging began. The facilitator simply instructed us to dance in free style. People started going crazy, arms flailing, twisting all over, hair flipping. I giggled to myself thinking they all looked so crazy. I was self-conscious so I moved back and forth a bit and swayed to the beat of the drums. My plan was to continue to sway, shut my eyes and enjoy the music. After a few minutes though, something inside of me yearned to increase my intensity. I transitioned to the "pony". I hopped back and forth on each leg, my head bouncing, and my shoulders in sync with each corresponding foot. I was not completely at ease at this point but was certainly getting more relaxed.

I glanced around the enormous room and there had to be several hundred people dancing. Very few were as conservative as me. I saw in their faces a complete lack of inhibition and a sense of freedom. Heck, I came here to be me and accept myself. I wanted to just be. So I closed my eyes and transformed into a cave girl. I started bouncing around like a lunatic-- totally out of my comfort zone but hell, I didn't know a soul in the room, and it felt awesome. It became increasingly hot and I noticed the outside door was ajar so I stepped out. It was drizzling but the cold water felt so refreshing on my sweaty hot face. I stayed outside even though I knew my hair would frizz in a million directions. I didn't care. There were others outside dancing and feeling uninhibited. I started losing myself and just allowed my body to go wherever. I bent down at my waist and just swung my arms like a monkey. I held my head and arms up to the sky and twirled around and around until I felt dizzy. I jumped, bounced, slumped, and twisted. My messed up hair was stuck to my face. The rain fell harder and I was exhilarated. My clothes and body were soaked. This was my true, authentic self. No guilt, no worry, no troubles. I did not care how I looked because it felt wonderful. Plus there were others there that looked just as nuts. This was an odd feeling I did not want to lose. I knew it was a breakthrough.

I danced for two hours that afternoon. Afterwards I went to my room, sat on the bed, fell over onto the clean, white sheets, laughed and felt wildly wonderful. I realized then that I have to embrace all things about myself.

When have you gone out of your comfort zone? How did it make you feel? If you are used to doing the same things all the time, try something new. Even if you are a little afraid, go for it. Sometimes the most wonderful experiences come out of stepping into the unknown.

The Inevitable But

When someone gives a compliment it should make us feel wonderful inside. But far too many times, folks will smile, say thanks and continue on with the inevitable "but"...

"Hey you lost weight. You look terrific!"

*"Thank you, **but** you haven't seen the cellulite on my thighs."*

"Your home is lovely."

*"Thanks, **but** don't look too closely, my sofa has stains."*

"Your kids are so polite."

*"Thanks, **but** you should be around them at bedtime."*

"Your hair is beautiful."

*"Thanks, **but** I wish it wasn't so curly and frizzy."*

"Your sweater looks so expensive."

*"Thanks, **but** I got it at a discount store for $2.00 in the clearance bin."*

"Your skin is so beautiful."

*"Thanks, **but** this is the one day when I don't have pimples all over my face."*

Strangely, accepting a compliment can be very challenging. For some unknown reason it is easier to accept negative comments.

Goodness knows there is enough negativity in the world and it would be life changing if we can readily accept kindness and let it sink in.

The next time you receive a compliment from someone, try this instead:

1)Look the person in the eyes and smile.

2)Say Thank you!

3)Take a breath. Say nothing more.

4)Receive the beautiful words.

5)Allow yourself to feel good.

The "buts" also work in another way:

*"Honey you did great out there in your fielding today, **but** you should not have swung at that horrible pitch in the last inning."*

*"Your report card looks great, **but** what about that B in science?"*

*"I'm so proud of you for having the courage to give your oral report in front of the class, **but** you should not have spoken so fast."*

*"It's wonderful that you won second place, **but** next time you should try for first place."*

Even with the best intentions, those "buts" can dash hopes and dreams and may lead to a belief that they are not good enough. The word "but" can negate anything positive that was said previously. If you have the most praiseworthy compliments coming out of your mouth and there is a "but" in there, it can wipe out all the good you were trying to convey.

Try saying what you want to say and leave out the "but". When compliments are given, stop at thank you. When you are saying something nice to someone else, stop before you say something negative. There is a time and a place for constructive comments, but I believe it will be better served during another conversation and not immediately after you say something encouraging. Be aware of the words that come out of your mouth. They can lift up or tear down.

Gayle Suzanne

Message In Massages

During my journey to please myself, I discovered the wonderful world of massage therapy. Here are a few memorable experiences:

My very first massage was at a school of massage. It was half the price of a regular massage in a spa. I was in the infant phase of doing things for myself, so I chose the least expensive route. I was greeted by a large man in his forties who stood 6'6' tall. His black hair was neatly tied in a foot-long pony tail. He had quite a large head, facial hair resembling Jackie Chan and wore a long white coat.

We entered the massage room and right in front of me was a single bed. He turned to the door and dead bolted it three times. Me, scary big man, three dead bolts and a bed. Yikes. I should not have been so cheap. He turned to me and said, "Please get undressed and I'll be back in a few minutes." He stepped into the next room through a swinging door. Inside that room were two other men smoking cigars (I kid you not.) I nervously removed most of my clothing and stood alone next to the bed in my bra and undies. Now what do I do? I forgot to ask my friends how much clothing to remove. It reminded me of my gynecology appointment and that important question, "Should I keep my socks on?"

I swung the door open a crack. "Hello. Excuse me. How much am I supposed to take off?"

I'm sure the two other cigar smoking men glanced at each other at that moment.

"As much as you feel comfortable in."

As I took a whiff of the stale cigar smoke, my decision was clear. I kept my underclothes on.

My large masseuse came back in, asked if I was ready and proceeded to pull the shades down. He lit a candle, clicked on Enya-like music and asked if I wanted oils or lotion. Oils it was! He advised me that oils might stain my clothing. Yeah, cheap ploy to get my clothes off, I thought.

"Nope I'm fine. Thanks."

As I was lying motionless on the bed covered with a thin sheet, I began taking some deep breaths to relax. I heard the faint voices of the men in the other room but as soon as the big scary man put his gigantic hands on my scalp and shoulders I fell into another dimension. It didn't take long for me to get in the zone. It was an hour long appointment and he spent about 15 minutes on my head and neck alone. By the time he moved down to my arms and shoulders, I realized I really did not want to ruin this particular bra, so I reached down, unclipped and flung it across the room and let him finish.

This was an important learning experience for me. I learned that my next massage would be from a woman so I would not have any angst at all, and chances are she would not be puffing on a cigar. I also learned that when the scalp is massaged with oil, it tends to make your hair stick up. There was no mirror in this room, so when I left I looked like the bride of Frankenstein.

Since then I have treated myself to all kinds of massages. Most have been fabulous but a few have been a little strange. I went to a gorgeous high end salon and the woman masseuse was very pleasant when I first met her. I told her I enjoy a gentle soft massage. She had good pressure but when she got to a knot or tight spot she would grunt a loud UGH. Her first grunt sounded like a burp so I smiled and tried to return to my trance, but she continued making that noise! After fifteen or so grunt-burps I asked her why she was making that noise. She replied that she made the noise to release my tight spots. Now, I'm no massage expert, but I am pretty sure that grunt-burping while massaging my knots will not loosen them any more effectively. I asked her to please stop because her noises were distracting. She did stop but then she started massaging me more deeply and it hurt.

One of my favorite places is this incredible spa in Connecticut. It is a top notch facility. You are provided with comfy big white robes and squishy flip flops. Inside is a sauna, steam room, whirl pool, indoor pool, full service spa services, all to use at your leisure for the day. They offer complimentary water, teas and fruit, a smoothie bar and two restaurants on the property.

On this visit I went alone and requested a 90 minute hot stone therapy treatment. After the massage I sauntered over to the quiet room to relax out and read. The area was dimly lit with twelve chaise lounge chairs surrounding the room. Each chair was covered with a thick navy blue micro fleece cushion. In the corner was an oversized lounge chair that was calling my name. That would be my spot for the next hour or so. I put the blanket over my feet, took a sip of my tea and began to read my book. Goodness knows how much time had passed before I woke up with a wee bit of drool on the left side of my mouth. Geez, the massage must have knocked me out! I laid still for a few seconds trying to wake up, and after a moment I sat up. I looked down. My entire left breast was hanging out exposed in full view for the other twelve loungers to see.

A few years ago I was ready to mix things up a bit. I requested an apple cinnamon bath followed by a hot stone massage. Only a piece of chocolate could make that combination any better. As I was in the room preparing for my bath, a stocky, robust, and fairly unattractive woman walked in and sprinkled the magical apple and cinnamon chunks in the tub. The water was the perfect temperature. I stepped in, closed my eyes and breathed in the scent of a freshly baked apple pie. A few minutes later I heard the door open again and Helga returned. She was carrying a loofah and a large brush with a handle. I looked down at all of my flesh and quickly realized there was not enough apple sprinkles in the tub to cover my privates. And there weren't any bubbles! I repositioned my hands and tried my best to cover the three things I desperately wanted to cover. She said she would start with my back. I leaned forward and let her begin. It felt scratchy and harsh, like my skin was being ripped off with sand. After a minute or so I was getting used to it and it was not too bad, until she moved forward and lifted my arms and scrubbed my armpits. She continued to brush my chest and my nether region. I had no choice but to pretend it wasn't happening. After she finished scraping me, I got out of the tub and took a shower (by myself). That was the quickest shower I ever took. I was just waiting for the door knob to move and watch her return and join me in the shower. Once I rinsed off, I walked to my massage room. I began to feel pieces of apple crisps in places where apple crisps should never be allowed.

Just Be

For most of my younger life and well into my thirties, I lived in a semi-state of rush and chaos. I had a lot of energy and never wanted to slow down. When I sat down it was only for a minute or two. My mind was constantly racing, thinking of the next thing I had to do. I had to keep productive. I lived this way for years. I would work, come home, take care of Becca and do laundry and make dinner and iron and vacuum, clean up the kitchen, get tomorrow's clothes ready, clean up around the house, go to the store, clean out a closet and then crash.

After my divorce, I went through a new found freedom phase and went pretty wild, full speed ahead. I had every other weekend and one night a week on my own while Becca was with her dad. On my free nights I would be out until the wee hours of the morning. I partied quite a bit and hung out with a group of friends who literally saved me after my divorce. They definitely came into my life for a season. I find it amazing how God brings people into our lives for just the perfect amount of time-- sometimes for a lifetime and sometimes for a brief time.

At age thirty-five, I realized that after a few years of going out constantly that I needed to grow up, learn how to be a big girl and stay home alone once in a while. I had to always be around people-- almost too much. I had a hard time staying alone with myself and I knew that there was work to be done because I knew deep down inside that going out night after night was not a healthy way to live. Could I be avoiding something?

I made a deal with myself that on the weekends when Becca was not with me, I would allow myself permission to go out one night but the other night I would stay home alone. I thought it would be good for me to spend time with myself and hopefully I would learn to love myself and enjoy my own company. Then, I would be able to relax and find peace and quiet within my soul.

The first few times I tried this, I made a list of things to do around the house. I have to admit I accomplished a lot! I was running around painting rooms, cleaning out closets, bagging up clothes, polishing woodwork, replacing tack paper, hanging pictures, cleaning out photo albums, moving things from one floor to another, ironing clothes, etc. Although those duties were positive and constructive, I was not finding much peace. I was literally running from myself by keeping so busy. I did not want to think of my circumstances and have to sort through deep rooted issues in order to heal my life. But I knew I had to, so I began to force myself to sit for a half hour in the quiet and just be.

The first time I tried this half hour silence, it was brutal. I remember after five minutes thinking that was an eternity. I was fidgety and wiggly. My fingers and toes were moving and I was shifting all over the place on the comfy couch. I was easily distracted, thinking about paying the mortgage or looking for a cat that I could play with. It reminded me of the Sponge Bob episode where SpongeBob was writing a school paper that he didn't want to write and he was totally distracted by the smallest thing. He would slide down in his chair and play with a pencil or a paperclip. He was so unfocused and wanted to do anything but complete that assignment. That's how I felt. I couldn't quiet my mind and concentrate.

It took me a while but I finally became content sitting alone in silence. I had some good cry sessions which were miserable but healing. I knew that my excessive running around was helping me avoid my painful and hurt feelings. The busier I was, the more I did not have to deal with my situation or myself. But I really didn't want to bury my head in the sand and ignore my issues. I have always been one to deal with things head on, but this was a hard period of time for me.

Now I savor my quiet time. I still have it today-- although not as much as I used to. My driving time is my quiet time most days. I use that time to talk to God, think of ways to be a blessing, and how to be okay with just being. Just be. I have to remind myself of that all the time. I am loved because of who I am, not for what I do.

Additionally, in order to just be, I have to embrace all of me. That includes my double chins, the cat hairballs in the cellar that I haven't had a chance to clean up, my impatience with the morning commute, the eight inch scar on my tummy that saved my life yet prevents me from being a swimsuit model, the irritation I feel when I'm around negative people, the lack of money to afford a second home, the inevitability of finding Christmas tree needles under the couch in August, the choice to eat cereal for dinner, and last night's dishes in the sink.

Take some time each day and sit quietly. Accept yourself and your circumstances exactly as they are in this moment. If you can only do it for one minute, that's okay. Just start.

Just be.

Gayle Suzanne

In The Midst Of Grand, Pay Attention To The Little Things

The awesomeness of the Grand Canyon is almost impossible to describe. The peaks and valleys of the carved rock; the way the sun hit the sides of the canyons at different times of the day, the sheer vastness of it, the magnitude of beauty. When my husband and I arrived at Grand Canyon National Park, we both agreed to experience the grandeur all at once rather than get a glimpse of it here and there. We did not want a tease. We walked a path to the canyon which was not far from the Visitors Center.

My expectation was that we would walk down a flight of stairs to a lookout of splendor. God would appear before me and I would be lifted to another dimension. I would find my purpose in life and be raised to a level of consciousness that I never could have imagined. I guess when you wait so long to experience a particular thing, expectations can get the best of you.

When we arrived at the lookout, the view was magnificent, that much was true. Beauty as far as the eye could see. It was literally breathtaking. But to get to the lookout we had to squeeze through a crowd of spectators. It wasn't serene like I envisioned, it was loud and chaotic.

One woman yelled to her husband "HANK, YA SHOULD SEE THE VIEW FROM OVA HEYA!"

Hank was only a few feet away from her and my ears were in between them both.

The yelling, people blocking my view, and children jumping and screaming off the rocks gave little to no chance of me hearing from the Creator Himself. In any other place this activity would not bother me as much, but for some reason I thought it would be a sacred spot where beauty was respected in SILENCE... or at least a place where people used their indoor voices. I cannot say that I was disappointed in the view because it was incredible, I just wished the grandness would have swept me away. I couldn't get in "the zone". Although I did find the zone in some other unexpected places:

- The feeling of free falling while on a helicopter tour of the Sedona canyons; the swooping in and out of the canyons was exhilarating.

- Smelling the Sedona pine trees as we were driving with the top down in our very slick, black convertible as we gazed up at a sky of twinkling stars.

- Laughing till my side hurt when my hubby jokingly suggested I buy a long scarf when we slid into the convertible (remember Isadora Duncan?).

- While visiting an energy vortex, I saw a woman riding her handsome horse. They appeared literally out of nowhere.

- Viewing the full moon through a telescope on a crystal clear night in Sedona and seeing the moon so close up that the craters looked touchable.

- Watching huge black birds soar solo above the Grand Canyon.

- Walking on our balcony in Sedona each morning and saying good morning to Snoopy Rock.

- Dipping my toes in the cool, clay-like bottom of the Colorado River-- as the outside temperature topped 102 degrees.

- Eating breakfast by the bubbling creek, sipping my mimosa, and watching the relaxed lives of the many ducks that passed by.

- Sitting outside ancient ruins and watching a delicate butterfly rest on my arm.

- Discovering a dime beneath my feet while visiting a vortex. Dimes have been a significant symbol since my mother's death earlier this year. This dime was a spiritual comfort to me.

After thinking about this amazing trip, I realized God's beauty is in the grand *and* the small. I have always been an observer of details. Little things can make something average into something spectacular. The statement that everything grand is the best is a misconception in my eyes. I *used* to believe that things on a larger scale mattered more, but as I mature and grow wiser, I realize it's in the little things where we can find the most happiness, contentment, joy, peace and love.

Gayle Suzanne

Life Unfolds The Way It Is Supposed To, Don't Give Up

Life can be full of disappointments, broken hearts, obstacles and challenges. Dealing with difficult situations can leave us feeling defeated and worn out. Things happen that we just don't understand. We try our best and things crumble around us. We struggle, suffer, experience pain but hold strong until our breakthrough comes. After enduring rough patches, I can understand how struggles are lessons in disguise. We are forced to grow, endure, dig deep and seek other solutions. Occasionally we learn that what we are striving for is not meant for us at all.

Here's an example. Years ago I was ready to change my career and start fresh. For over a decade, I volunteered for a non-profit organization performing various tasks where I gained valuable experience. I felt that this was my new calling. It would mean a cut in pay but I felt confident the different kind of work would be rewarding and fulfilling! I applied for all types of jobs. I wanted to help people. My heart was in the right place. I was determined to find my place.

Over the next few months several of the companies I applied to replied with unpleasant news: Not enough experience. Overqualified. We offered the position to someone else. It stung, but I brushed it off and continued applying. If only I could get an interview, then I could sway them with my charm.

I finally found a position that looked terrific. It was challenging, had great benefits, a perfect commute, and the company had a great reputation. I applied and was convinced this was the perfect job for me. A few days later I checked my email before leaving for work. *Nope not interested.* Are you kidding me? I banged the delete key and my hissy fit began.

As soon as I jumped in the driver's seat and slammed the door, I screamed: "God, can You throw me a bone here? I am so sick of getting rejected! That was the job *I wanted!* I know You know because I prayed for that job! Would You give me a break *and do what I want for once*?"

Yeah, I know, quite harsh.

That commute was a doozy. I ranted and raved and yelled and wailed and griped and complained. My hands were up in the air flailing all over the place. I have no doubt I looked like a lunatic to other drivers. I didn't care. I felt duped. My motives were in the right place. I wanted to help, I was willing to make less money. As I pulled into my work parking lot, I calmed down, reapplied my makeup, took a few deep breaths, and reluctantly walked into work. I finally made peace with the big guy and surrendered.

"Okay God, apparently this job is not in Your plan for me. I will be open to do *Your* will. Please use me as you wish so I fulfill Your will. Please use me as a *vessel*."

HUH? I don't even know where that word came from. Seriously, it just fell out of my mouth. I can say with certainty that "vessel" is not a word that I usually use as part of my vocabulary. I wanted HIM to know that I wanted to do His will and for Him to use me in His way - whatever that is.

"God use me as a vessel. God use me as a vessel. God use me as a vessel." Mumbling this foreign talk, I walked through the door directly to my desk.

Within a minute after taking off my coat, one of my co workers popped in and asked if I would have breakfast with her. I said sure. We sat down and she instantly began telling me about a personal problem she was struggling with. She needed someone to talk to. Guess it didn't take Him long to find a willing participant.

Is this what listening to God is all about? Just being open to someone in need? Taking a few moments to be there for someone who is going through a rough time? Is this what being a vessel means? Is He looking for me to open my heart and mind and be there for someone else?

I probably got more satisfaction out of those moments talking with her than being hired for that dream job. Once we finished up our conversation I could see that a huge weight had been lifted from her shoulders. I just listened. An attentive friend appeared to be exactly what she needed. I was glad to be there for her and wondered if that was really what God intended me to do that day. I think I might have been her vessel.

That was on a Thursday. On Saturday, my daughter, Becca, and I went into a random nail salon a few towns away for a pedicure. Next to us was a sweet young woman getting a manicure. She shared that she was going to a gala event that evening for work. I asked where she worked and she named my dream job company. Wow. Continuing on with our conversation, she shared that she worked in the *same department as the job I applied for*! I told her that I saw a job posting online. She said that she does the exact same thing. One of her coworkers left the company and they were looking for someone to fill her position.

Here's the kicker: I asked her how she liked it. She said the boss was difficult to work for and the job entailed a lot of running around and grunt work. She worked many nights and weekends. It was not as glamorous as it seemed. She was burnt out.

BAM!

I believe God has a good plan for our lives. That coincidental encounter convinced me that God will close the doors that are not right for me. I also hold onto faith that He will open the right door. It most likely will not be in my timing. I choose to believe that when a door does open, it will be His will – not mine. I just have to learn to let go of *my* will.

Dear God, please open the right door for me and close the wrong door, so I don't have to make a difficult decision determining if it is Your will or not.

This is my practical, lazy prayer. When I pray for something that I want, I don't want to have to think about making the right decision. Sometimes opportunities arise and I am not sure what to do. So I pray for God to shut all the doors that are not His will. This might mean a lot of rejection, but it means I can trust the doors that actually open. I have to trust that the right door will open in His time, which of course will not be in my timing. I guess God, the universe, or something greater than me knew that position was not the right fit for me. I dusted myself off and moved on.

A short time passed and I enrolled in a coaching certification program. After the first weekend of class I knew *this* was my calling. Coaching was in my bones. But it was not an easy year. I had scheduled two hour teleconferences for 30+ weeks, hours of coaching between peers, mentor coaching, small groups, specialized groups, book reports, e-books and complimentary sessions all while working at my full time job, household duties (although limited as I don't cook, clean the house or do yard work). Some nights I was so exhausted that all I wanted to do was crawl in bed at 7pm and cozy up with my kitties and a squishy pillow, but I had a two hour conference call which would last until 10pm. I had to be awake and attentive.

Were there moments I wanted to give up? Absolutely! I could not throw in the towel. So during the most hectic and overwhelming sections of the class I rearranged my schedule and said yes to the things that were of the utmost importance and said no to everything else. My social life became non-existent, but I did what I had to do.

After I became certified (the good kind), I slept for three days. My work was done! I anticipated that the phone would ring off the hook and hundreds of people would line up outside my front door begging me to take them on as clients.

No calls, no line. Maybe this was all for nothing? I did not want to force my business with hooks and sales pitches, I wanted it to come naturally. I had a deep desire to help. I was fortunate that I did have a few wonderful clients but I worried that I was not flourishing the way I "should" be. I prayed to God, planted seeds and informed others about my new endeavor. Then I let it go. It was time for God to do His part.

No exaggeration – three days later I received an email from a non-profit director who was interested in what I had to offer. After a pleasant phone conversation I booked a six session workshop! She prayed for someone like *me* to come along! Within the next two weeks I scheduled four more speaking engagements.

Life will hand out disappointments, wrong turns, and outcomes we think are wrong. Push through, do not give up, the right door will eventually open. Life unfolds the way it is meant to.

Boundaries

Boundaries. No one is going to set them for you. It is completely up to you to develop healthy boundaries. I had to find a healthy way to determine what was other people's stuff and what was my stuff. There was a time when I took on the responsibility for everything, I mean *everything*. If someone was randomly moody, it had to be my fault. If someone was upset about something, it had to be my fault. If someone was unkind to me, it had to be that I was a loser. If someone was bitchy and rude, it had to be me to apologize. If someone was snappy, I had to pick up the pieces and make them happy. I did not know who I was. I just thought that I was someone who was the cause of all bad things and someone who was just a punching bag for others to take their frustrations out on. I always thought people were mad at me. And I constantly asked if they were.

Without boundaries set in my life, I did not know where I began and others ended. I people-pleased and did what others wanted so I could be accepted, regardless of how it made me feel. I cannot be totally harsh on myself. That was who I was at the time. I had to evolve and grow. I look back and some of the toughest relationships I had were some of the ones I am most grateful for. They hurt but the pain I went through made me search inside myself and forced me to make some pretty big changes. First and foremost, I had to stop apologizing for who I was. I had to realize that people are responsible for their own moods, inappropriate behavior, and decisions. I had to learn, little by little, that I am not responsible for everyone's actions. It took me a long time to "get" this. I thought by people pleasing and apologizing and taking the heat all the time, I was doing a good thing for the relationship. But that mindset was hurting me. I was taking on a bunch of stuff that was not mine to begin with. I had to let some stuff go-- some stuff that had been a part of me for years. I had to start living a new way.

Beginning the boundary process for me meant 1) taking a stand for something I believed in, 2) not taking responsibility for other's actions, and 3) learning to do what was best for me without hurting or offending anyone else in the process. This was not easy for me to do in the beginning. When people would say something insensitive to me, I got flustered when I told them how I felt. My voice would go up three octaves and I would whine and get upset. Years later, I have learned to calmly, and with love (trying with love anyways) to tell them how I feel without judgment or getting upset. It is a process. Sometimes even now I will get sweaty or hot when I have to confront someone. But I am not as fearful as I used to be.

I remember starting with small issues and with people that I loved and knew loved me. If something happened that I was uncomfortable with, I would say something to them in a small way and preface by saying something positive. So if I had to set a boundary with a coworker who was always late, which in turn made me late for a meeting, I'd said, "I'm so glad we joined this committee together. I would like to try and leave a bit earlier so we aren't late for the meetings. If that is too early for you to arrive, then we might have to take separate cars and I'll meet you there. How does that sound?" In this situation, I am taking care of myself and giving her the option to either arrive on time or go on her own. Either way, I'm taking care of myself.

It was hard for me to do this. I was not used to sitting in the discomfort of confrontation. I had given in for so many years because I wanted to keep the peace. It was hard to say what I really wanted. The old me would have said, "Oh it's okay, you can be late whenever you want and make me late. It's okay. I'll be fine if I get fired." Secondly, no one was used to this behavior coming from me. They were not used to me saying no and early on a common response was, "Oh Gayle you're too sensitive". When others started to get used to the changed me-- I felt a backlash of anger and frustration on their end. I'm sure they wanted me to take responsibility again. I knew I had to stick to my guns. I had to set limits in every area of my life. I was being walked all over and I had to start with small issues with the safe loving people in my life. Then I moved on to those who might reject me forever.

And there were plenty of them. Even so, I can say no today and calmly set loving boundaries that will benefit me and others.

Gayle Suzanne

Angels-- They're All Around Us

When Becca was in middle school, she began having problems with her heart. Randomly during soccer practice or running track, she would feel her heart beat rapidly. Her chest hurt, her vision became distorted and she had trouble standing up. We went to a cardiologist on and off over a three year period and each time she was given a halter monitor to track the episodes. But when she wore that halter, her heart rate would be normal. It took almost three years to detect her condition. Her heart rate was 257 beats per minute, which even raised the eyebrows of the cardiologist. Now we had a definite diagnosis and could move forward with a treatment.

She had something called Supra-ventricular Tachycardia or SVT (thank God for acronyms). This heart condition is most commonly due to a loop of electrical current in the heart, which as it loops, causes the heart to beat quickly. Her type of SVT was an AV nodal reentrant tachycardia. This type of condition, when left untreated, could result in serious injury or even death. Luckily we knew what we were dealing with now-- she would have to have an ablation procedure.

The procedure would be performed at Children's Hospital in Boston. I had never been to Children's Hospital and did not know anyone there. Thank goodness I had my GPS or else I would not even know how to get there. I was in the dark about everything and felt pretty uneasy about the whole situation. Her local cardiologist said this would be a routine procedure and she would be just fine. But this was a *heart* procedure, not removing a splinter.

Understandably, I was nervous and anxious. I knew I would not be calm until the procedure was over and she was okay.

A few days after I found out about her surgery, I was invited to a surprise wedding shower for a very dear friend of mine. I didn't believe I would know many people attending and was honestly on overload with all I had on my mind. I had this fear rattling around in my head, along with all the "What if's?" and the unknowns. I knew I had to put my angst aside for her wedding shower, but my whole being was scared and anxious. On the way to the shower I prayed to God to help me enjoy the day and not worry. Help me put on a big smile and keep the focus on my lovely friend.

When I arrived it turned out I knew several women there, and some I had not seen since college and boy, did they look awesome! I sat next to an adorable woman who was a childhood friend of the bride. Her name was Karen. She was simply a joy to talk with-- vivacious and open and just a love bug. Karen was disappointed that she would be out of town on vacation during the wedding. She randomly shared that she worked at Children's Hospital in Boston. My ears perked up and I was compelled to spill my guts about Becca's heart procedure. I casually asked her if she knew the surgeon. I figured it was a long shot, but maybe she had heard something about him. Turned out she worked *for* him for over twenty years!

Karen **was** my angel that day. She explained the details of the procedure and confirmed that the doctor was highly skilled and reputable. The mountain of worry on my shoulders diminished as I clung to every supportive word she said. Amazing. Words cannot describe the comfort she provided me with that day. Karen went so far as to tell each person on duty the day of the surgery to take extra good care of my daughter. And boy they did! Karen also called me during the procedure to check in. She was a Godsend.

Karen, thank you. I might never see you again but just want you to know you are in my heart forever.

If you think there are no angels, I'm sorry, but I will lovingly have to disagree.

Gayle Suzanne

Incense, Stinky Cheese, And The Crisp White Sheet

After my divorce and during a whining session with my therapist, she suggested I attend a seminar on healing and holistic techniques. She knew that I was having a horrible time with my self esteem and maybe these meditation based seminars would help me see myself differently.

Amy was the facilitator at my first Reiki seminar. Reiki is hands-on body work healing. She had me at hello. Immediately I set up a private appointment with her, which happened to be one week before my divorce court date. This was the drive-through dose of relaxation tips I needed to get me through the next week. Little did I know it would change my entire life.

I was intrigued by the whole holistic approach to things, but it was so foreign to me I didn't have a clue what to expect. All I really knew was I was going to dig deep emotionally and I had to have courage to do this. I didn't necessarily want to run away, but I wasn't sure how far I wanted to go. I knew it could be a gut wrenching experience. As I sat in the waiting room in Amy's office, I glanced around and saw several Buddha statues. There was a strong smell of incense in the room and large pillows scattered around on the floor and on the couch and chairs. Homey, inviting, beautiful and soothing, yet I was so uncomfortable.

Amy greeted me. She was quite lovely and peaceful looking. Short brown hair, flawless skin, perfectly toned body. She was obviously at ease in her own skin and serenity oozed out of her. She had a strong English accent and asked me politely to remove my shoes before entering another room. As I took off my shoes, I realized they were the sandals that made my feet sweat and smell like stinky cheese. I removed my shoes and buried my toes in her shag carpet in an attempt to mask any odor. I followed her into her studio and there were huge soft pillows in each corner of the room, more incense and waterfall music playing softly in the background. In the center of the room was a cot with a crisp white sheet and a fluffy pillow on top.

She motioned for me to sit next to her on one of the big pillows on the floor.

"Hello Gayle. Can you tell me why you are here?" Amy calmly asked. I loved her accent and wished she would just continue talking so I didn't have to bare my soul.

"I separated from my husband about 6 months ago. I'm sad and depressed all the time and I want to be loved by a man but I don't think I'm ready for a relationship. My heart hurts so much it feels like I'm breaking apart. I'm so lonely. I'm not sure I'll be able to be in a healthy relationship. I don't have a good opinion of myself and I want to learn to love myself. I want to be whole on my own before entering into a relationship and at the same time I think there is something wrong with me because I am not dating anyone now. I'm all over the place emotionally and so unhappy and need help."

I finally took a breath. She wasn't laughing and looked at me with kind and loving eyes.

I am in the right place.

Amy explained the process of Reiki. She told me that I would lie down on the table and she would be sending light and love to each of my chakras. The chakras are focal points in your body where some past harmful experiences could be stored. I guess I wanted them to be unblocked and I wanted to live freely. The purpose of Reiki as I understood it, is to release the pain of earlier memories so love can flow with the energy of your body. As we were talking face to face, Amy asked me to pick a very painful event in my life. She told me to as far back as I could remember. I picked a scary event of my childhood when I was about four years old. It was a time when I was scared and felt unloved and unlovable. We would be working with that memory during this session.

This is heavy shit.

She asked me to lie down on the table and she covered me with a crisp, white sheet. I was momentarily sidetracked by the thought of my stinky feet, but I guess if they smelled that bad she could simply put another sheet or pillow over them...or she could move the incense closer to my feet. Either way I was not going to worry about it. I closed my eyes and tried to relax.

She gently talked to me as she placed her hands on my belly. *Relax your scalp, your nose, your eyes, your spine, your stomach, your waist, your buttocks, your legs and your toes.* She helped me imagine a submarine style door on the top of my head and asked me to open it up. She guided me. Two corks were stuck to the bottom of my feet and I pulled them both out. She talked me through. She had me visualize a bright light gently enter the opening at the top of my head and penetrate slowly throughout my body. My body felt warm as the light hit each part of my body. I felt each section of me heat up. I fell into a deep state of relaxation-- kind of like a trance. Any negative emotion or feeling left my body through the two small holes at the bottom of my feet. In minutes, my body felt light and free and full of good feelings. I was on my way to the unknown. It wasn't scary, it felt absolutely wonderful.

Amy told me to think back early in my childhood, as far back as I could go, and think of my most painful memory. As I thought of the memory, she asked me to *feel* the memory. At first I thought about the memory and my mind switched to something else immediately. I did not want to go there. I did not want to FEEL what was there. But I went to the memory because I wanted to heal in the right way. Amy's hands cupped my face. I thought of the memory.

I was four. I was in my living room with my older sister and parents. My mother and father were in a huge fight. Daddy left the house. I ran to the window and watched him leave. I was terrified as I saw him drive away. I thought he was going to leave us and I would never see him again. I loved my daddy so much and did not want him to leave. I curled up in the closet and cried. I was completely terrified.

I went there. It took me a while to get there but once I did, I was there. Mind, body, spirit. I was four-years-old again. I pictured the room around me, the colors, the furniture, the curtains, the coffee table-- everything came back to me in my mind. It did not feel good. I felt the horror and the vulnerability of this sweet chubby little kid. To me it was not me, just some poor little girl. My four-year-old self and current self were detached at this point, although I did feel her pain and had compassion for her. Unexpectedly, the tears started pouring out of me and down the sides of my face. The crisp white sheet became stained with black marks and wet tear spots. Amy gently told me to stay with it-- stay with my feelings. Just be there with it all. She handed me tissues and I cried, but not loudly. I sobbed from the deepest part of me. Every minute or so I would regain composure and try to breathe deeply so I wouldn't hyperventilate. Amy's hands moved to my heart. She was in tune with my body. My heart hurt so much but at the same time so much was being released out of me.

Amy asked me to take my four-year-old self to a safe beautiful place of my choosing. I pictured her in the forest. She was sitting on a log next to a flowing stream with her feet dangling in the clear bubbly water. She wore a white lace flowing dress with an eyelet pattern. The sky was blue and crystal clear. There were several butterflies fluttering around. The stream was narrow and flowed gently over the rocks that were covered with moss. She sat on the log and looked down at her feet. The innocence about her was astounding. A little chubby girl with bright blue eyes with a deep love of life but was so sad with a crushed spirit. She was missing several front teeth but her smile lit up a room. Her hair was brown in a little pixie haircut. Her cheeks were plump and adorable just waiting to be pinched.

Now it was time to comfort her. Amy asked me to ask my higher power, whoever I chose that to be, to fill me up with love and comfort for this little girl. I thought about the options I had. I could pick God Himself or Mary or Jesus. I asked Jesus to come to the scene. He came to her and simply looked at her with love-- so much love. He sat down beside her, lifted her up and placed her on His lap. He just held her. She hugged him back. It was pivotal for me to stay in this moment. I watched Him hold her and just love her quietly. An insane wave of comfort overcame my body.

I have no words to describe this feeling. It was a movie in my mind, so clear and vivid. What a beautiful scene. It was so quiet, so real and I felt like I was right there experiencing a love that I have never felt before. I craved more.

I immediately stopped crying and felt this huge sense of love and serenity. I knew right then and there that God loved me. He loved ME! I lingered with this feeling. Although I was raised Catholic and went to mass on Sundays I never felt that kind of love. I never really tapped into the feeling that God really loved ME. I felt that He loved other people, the chosen ones of the world, the beautiful people, the successful ones, but not a defective loser like me. This day was a turning point for me. I actually felt that love. If I put my faith in this feeling my life would never be the same.

Amy then asked me, the thirty-four-year-old woman lying under the crisp white sheet, to join my four-year-old inner child. She also asked me to request the presence of the One who was giving her light and love. Adult me entered the scene. Amy told me to embrace the four-year-old girl and to look at her very closely. I walked up to her and smiled. I looked her in the eyes and into her soul. Amy asked me to think about what I saw in that little girl. For the first time in my life that little girl was precious to me. She was beautiful. Jesus was right there with both of us, showing us love.

Monumental moment.

I was thirty-four and wanted to be loved. She was four and wanted to be loved. God loves me. He loved me at age four and He loves me now.

I can give that kind of love to myself. I did not need a man to love me right now. I needed to get in touch with that kind of love within myself and with my higher power. I had to love myself the way I was loved in that moment. For me, tapping into that love for myself was when I would be whole and ready to enter into a relationship.

I began seeing Amy every other week for one year after that. We did some phenomenal work. I healed so much in those sessions. I no longer feel worthless and defective.

Gayle Suzanne

Out Of Body Experience

In my early twenties, I began attending a twelve step program because it was time to deal with my co-dependency issues. I was unhappy and unsatisfied. I was aware that I relied heavily on people to make me happy. Their mood and wants determined my mood and wants. If someone was happy, I was happy. If they were sad, I thought I did something to upset them. If they were mad, I thought I did something to make them angry. I was emotionally exhausted. Deep down I knew I had some serious unresolved issues and thought this was an excellent place to start.

One night we had a particularly intense meeting and afterwards I had a gut wrenching talk with my sponsor. We dug deep and I was able to expose my innermost core issues with her. I purged unhealthy junk that was taking up space in my head. The conversation was quite disturbing but I knew it was cleansing and essential for my growth. I was unsettled when I arrived home but as the hours passed I was fine. I went to bed at 10 PM and woke up around 2 AM not feeling well. My body was shaking from head to toe. My teeth were chattering and my hands were trembling. Every ounce of me was twitching. I tried to go back to sleep, but being agitated and uncomfortable, I kept tossing and turning. I tried deep breathing and meditating to quiet my thoughts. The shaking was uncontrollable. I took my temperature as I thought I had a fever, but no such luck. I went back to bed and still felt shaky all over. I was frightened because I did not have a clue what was wrong with me.

After an half hour or so, I got up again and walked to the kitchen in the dark. I sat down at the table and laid my head down, resting it on my folded arms. I was scared. I didn't know what was wrong with me and never felt this feeling before. I had been shaking for over a half hour at this point. I drank a glass of water and had a piece of cheese and started praying. Drink, eat, pray. I didn't know what was happening but felt like I was going to pass out. I asked Jesus to help me. Please take this awful feeling away. My entire head was shaking and bobbing up and down the table - even though my arms were under my head for protection I was banging against the table. The severity of my shaking was not going away. It was so intense and raw.

After several minutes of hard praying (almost plead-praying if there is such a thing) I felt something at the top of my head. I put my hand on my head to see if something mysteriously landed there, but there was nothing there. It felt like a thick liquid was slowly being poured on my head. I remained still as I felt the heavy liquid begin to drip down the sides of my face. It continued down my forehead. I touched my head and face to feel what the substance was, but it was just my hair and skin. As soon as the syrupy substance hit each part of my face and head, the shaking completely stopped. It was amazing. I still had my head down on the table and felt such comfort in the thick, healing syrup. When it hit my shoulders, I felt some kind of presence in the room; something beyond me that I simply cannot describe. I had a visual of Jesus and for about ten seconds He was with me. If I was reading this about someone else, I would think they were crazy. Had I not experienced it personally, I would not have truly believed this could happen. I have never felt His presence before. I was convinced that he was healing me at that moment. I felt tremendous peace. Nothing would harm me. God was with me. I felt Him say, "All will be okay, come to Me." Then the feeling, the vision, whatever it was – disappeared. I cannot put into words how I felt. I was so blessed to have this experience. I stayed still until the last of the liquid reached my feet. I was not afraid. I wanted Him back again. I actually tried to force the presence back, but it did not work. Almost in a daze, I got up and went back to bed. As soon as I hit the pillow I was out. I can only imagine that I was in utter peace.

That experienced solidified my faith. I will never question whether God exists. I know that He does.

The Replacement Test

Years ago when I was agonizing about a decision I had to make, I learned about the replacement test. This test has guided me through some very difficult times in my life. It was most effective when I was in a bad place emotionally. I am forever grateful for this tool.

It goes like this. When you are at a crossroad about a decision you have to make and you are not sure what the right thing to do is, replace yourself in the same situation with someone you love unconditionally. Think of how you would advise that person in the exact situation. Now, you might be asking yourself "Why do this? I am perfectly capable of making my own choices". The thing is that sometimes we might not feel good enough about ourselves or love ourselves enough in that moment to make the *best* decision for ourselves...and the decision we might end up with could cause us more heartache in the long run.

I select my daughter when I'm ready to take the replacement test. I find a comfortable place to sit across from another chair or sofa. I take a few deep breaths and actually visualize her sitting across from me even though she's not really there. I review the pros and cons of the situation. Most times I will write the good, bad and ugly of the situation on a pad of paper. This helps me clearly evaluate the situation as it really is. With my eyes shut, I am quiet for a moment. Sometimes the moment turns into an hour or two. I picture the whole scenario as if it is happening to her. I visualize my daughter being in the exact same situation. I ponder what the *best solution is for her in the long run*. It might cause pain or be a hard thing to do initially, but in the end it is the healthiest decision.

That is my answer.

No matter what my state of mind is, this test works for me because I am giving advice as someone who loves her unconditionally. Any decision I make for myself in this way is the right one because that decision is made with pure love.

Try the replacement test for a minor or life altering decision. It just might be the way to give you the clarity you need to move forward in a gentle, loving, positive way.

Eliminate Those Limiting Beliefs!

Limiting beliefs are negative thoughts that we live by that somewhere along the way have become our truths. We all have dreams of what can be, but sometimes our limiting beliefs hold us back from going after what we really want and desire.

When I first learned of this concept, I have to admit, I had a hard time uncovering just one limiting belief about myself. They can be so embedded in our unconscious mind that we have to really cut ourselves wide open to discover them.

Here is one personal example of a limiting belief. During the initial stages of writing this book, I was going along just fine. Ideas were flooding my mind and I did not have enough time in the day to put on paper all the things I wanted to write about. Then I hit the halfway point. I became stuck. I lost motivation, I would procrastinate over the simplest tasks, my creative juices stopped flowing. I could not get out a drip. I was done writing. I had nothing left to say.

I think once I got to the point where I really felt I could publish a book and this could actually happen, panic set it. I began to doubt. Who would buy a book written by me? I am an unknown, a nobody. What if I publish and only loved ones buy it? And what if some of my friends and family don't buy it? I'm not a famous author, I'm just wasting my time. I'm ordinary, who will care what I have to say? I am from a small town and do not know anyone famous to help me. I have been through so much pain and suffering, who would want to read about that? No one will get it if they read it. People who love me will buy it because they feel sorry for me. I'm not a supermodel so when they see my face on the little box on the outside cover, others will put the book down because they don't like how I look.

All of these statements were limiting beliefs. They were keeping me from where I wanted to go. They were keeping me down, emotionally and physically. Limiting beliefs can stop us dead in our tracks. These unwarranted thoughts may keep us stuck for years in a place where we really do not want to be. They keep us safe from "failure" and might deter us from following our dreams and pursuing what our true God given purpose is in life.

There are so many limiting beliefs that we place on our lives:

- There are no good single people out there, I'm going to be alone the rest of my life.

- I couldn't possibly do that, I'm not smart enough.

- I don't have the proper education.

- Even though I hate my job, I won't look for another one because no one will hire me.

- I could never go back to school at my age.

- I'm not pretty enough.

- I'm not thin enough.

- I have to work harder to be seen as equal to everyone else.

These are real thoughts and feelings that some of us might have at our core. We generally do not share these beliefs over coffee with a neighbor-- they are ingrained in us. We accept them to be truth. We may not even be aware that they exist.

The thing is, they are not truth. You might think it is your truth, but it is not THE truth. It is up to us to be aware of what beliefs are holding us back from what we really want and to turn them around.

For me, I had to retrain my brain to think differently about publishing this book. I made an affirming statement to myself. Even though I am not famous I am writing with 100% effort and passion. I believe in the content of this book and will publish it in the hope that it will help someone. I want to share hope, laughter and love with others. I have no control over the outcome of sales. Whether this book sells or not is not an indicator of success or failure on my part. I'll put forth my best and that is all I can ask of myself.

What this did for me was life changing. It took the pressure off the end result and released my blocks. Almost instantly my mind became free and my creativity was ignited. Once I worked through this, my writing began to flow. The affirming statements helped me believe that my self-worth was not dependent on the sale of the book.

Instead of those limiting beliefs, try these statements instead:

- Yes there is a perfect partner for me.

- I might not be perfect but God loves me just as I am,

I should too!

- I've never done this before but I'll give it my best try.

- I am going to apply for this position and see what happens.

- I'm going to network and apply for jobs until I get the one I want.

- If I try to organize my time, I can go back to school.

- I have so many gifts and talents.

Take a few minutes and write down one of your limiting beliefs. Figure out when you started to feel that way. Was it something you learned in childhood? Something you learned in school? Something a mean kid said to you?

Make a positive statement out of your limiting belief. Repeat until it sinks in and you really believe the positive affirmation. It is so freeing to release those beliefs. It will give you hope and open the doors for a better future!

PART 3

Divorce and Relationships

Dating And Rejection

Dating and rejection, those are two words that sometimes go hand in hand. If you put yourself out there and begin dating, you might find yourself at the receiving end of some hurtful situations. No one likes rejection but maybe we can look at it in a different way.

When I was dating in my mid-thirties, I went through some ups and downs. My first date after my divorce was with a handsome man whom I met on Match.com. We chatted online for several weeks and decided to meet in a well lit public place (I know the rules). He was on time and we sat at the bar of a pub-style restaurant. We laughed and talked about ourselves, work, life, kids, goals, what we wanted in life. The vibe was effortless and the conversation flowed smoothly. As we winded down and with no prompting of my own, he asked for my number and said he'd love to see me again. He kissed me on the cheek and said I'd hear from him soon. I felt like I hit the jackpot on the first date! Search is over-- phew! Dating was not so bad after all.

As I was driving home, the evening replayed in my mind. Great eye contact, nice back and forth conversation, no awkward silences, flirting by him, giggling by me. We had silly and serious moments. It was a perfect evening! When I arrived home I sent him a charming thank you email. After all, he was the perfect gentleman and paid for the appetizers. I was excited to see him again.

After I forwarded my note, I saw his name pop up within a few minutes. He replied so fast! He must have been waiting to hear from me!

"Nice to meet you, but I'm not interested in you."

What?

I read it again. *"...not interested in you."* What?

Rejection?

I didn't get it. Just a few short hours ago he laughed with me, shared personal thoughts with me, he flirted, he asked for my number, he said he wanted to see me again. All of these things were his words, not coerced by me. He said them without hesitation.

The tears poured down my face.

My immediate thoughts: *What was wrong with me? Why didn't he like me? Did I turn him off? Am I repulsive? Was I boring? I'm not pretty enough. I should have had sex with him in the parking lot. Why am I such a loser? I'm never going to be loved. I'm not loveable. I'm defective.*

Some time passed and I completed my self-torture. I settled down and thought things through a little more. Since my divorce, I had spent a lot of time and energy improving my self worth and self esteem. I learned to treat myself with gentleness and kindness. The questions and thoughts that were going through my mind after his email were not loving thoughts and did not serve my highest good. Those thoughts were hurting me.

After I dried my tears I was ready to think rationally. I was determined that I wasn't going to allow a person to make me feel like crap about myself-- especially someone I had only met a few hours ago!

I decided to make a list of my truths. These thoughts would serve my highest good.

Truth #1. Sometimes people tell you things that you want to hear that are not necessarily the truth. He probably felt more comfortable saying that he'll call rather than saying he's not interested. That is his issue and it has nothing to do with me. I'm a big girl and encourage honesty, even if it might sting a bit.

Truth #2. I can go on a date and have a great time! I don't have to marry the guy or even see him again. I can have fun in the moment without expectations. I'm fortunate that I had a nice night with him. Nothing came of it, but the night was pleasant and I could hold my own!

Truth #3. Just because one man was not interested in pursuing a relationship with me does not mean I am not worthy of being in a healthy relationship.

Truth #4. Sometimes people are just not a match. It does not mean that one is any better or less than the other, it just means that they are not a good fit. There have been many wonderful men that I've met that were not for me. Not because they were losers, but because the chemistry between us was not there. They would make a wonderful partner for someone else, but not me. The same thing goes for them. They might have thought I was a great person, but I wasn't a match for them. That makes it so much easier for me to handle rejection. I looked at it this way: if I went out with someone who was a great man, but there were no sparks and I did not want to go out with him again,

I certainly would not want him to feel badly about himself. I would not want to lead him on either, so saying you are nice but I truly don't think we would work out should not make him feel bad about himself. Just because someone does not want to go out with me, it does not mean that I am not worthwhile or an appealing person. It just means I'm not for *him*. Simple as that!

Truth #5. I am not going to give away all of my power. As I reviewed the evening, it dawned on me that I was so concerned about what he thought of me, that I really did not pay much attention to how he made me feel and what I thought of him. Did HE make me laugh? Nah, not too much. Did HE make me feel special and attractive? A little bit, but not really. Did HE impress me? I guess, but probably with his good looks more than anything else. When I dated after that, I thought in terms of what I wanted, rather than if he wanted me. Things shifted after that and my attitude really changed. I became the interviewer rather than the interviewee. Was he what I was looking for? Did he have the qualities I wanted in a relationship?

I do not like the term "dump". When someone "dumps" someone else, the connotation is that the dumper is superior to the dumpee. I choose not to look at dating like that. It either works or it does not. No one is better than the other. Just different. That helped me so much through this process. By having this mindset, I was able to keep my confidence level up even when I was interested in someone and they were not interested in me. I would have my moments of disappointment but I'd feel the hurt, shake myself off and move on. I was not about to let anyone steal the peace and self worth I worked so hard to attain.

If He's At The Bar And Looks Like Liberace, He's Gotta Be My Blind Date

After my divorce, I reflected a lot on my marriage and although it was sad that our marriage ended, I truly felt gratitude for all that I gained from our time together. We had a beautiful daughter and I became part of his wonderful family. I also gained an incredible new "mother", who I remain very close with to this day.

It took a few years to figure out what I really wanted in life. After some growth spurts, I figured I'd take a shot and dip in the dating pool. Dating again in my thirties was something I dreaded.

I started on Match.com. Honestly, I met some very decent men through this service. I tried to keep an open mind and even if someone was really different than me, I made an effort to see commonalities and the good in him.

Unfortunately, I can't say that about all of them.

Ray - While on the salad course of our blind date he told me he was ready to be exclusive with me. I had just placed a cherry tomato in my mouth and almost spit it across the room. How can anyone be certain at the salad that you want to be committed? I'm not sure how others feel but to me, exclusivity comes after at least a few dates.

Joe - This was a fix-up. Joe was forty-five minutes late for our blind date. I waited outside the restaurant where we agreed to meet. He arrived and opened the door for himself and walked in the restaurant in front of me. I almost walked through the glass door when it closed in my face. Before our drinks arrived he explained what he did for business. He was self made and apparently, quite wealthy. He told me that he had such a hard time finding the right girl because they were all interested in his money. He was looking for someone who wanted him for him and not for his mattress stash. For over an hour he talked about his money... how much he had... how he made it... what he does with it... how successful he was... how much he travels... how money smells. I can't be certain but I think midway through the date he forgot my name.

Bill - A female acquaintance of mine fixed us up on a double date. We met at her home on the lake and went for a boat ride. The night started out promising. It was a beautiful summer night and the lake was crystal clear. When we docked Bill and I had a minute to talk and he told me a little about his failed relationship. Out of nowhere he asked if I would ever consider wearing whipped cream underwear (yeah I can't make this stuff up). After the boat ride we sat around a campfire. Bill smoked pot all night while the other two did cocaine and popped pills. It was most certainly an early night for me.

Peter - He swore during the entire date, watched the game on the overhead television, did not ask a thing about me and was lewd in his topics. This is where I learned and perfected my "run in the parking lot" goodbye. We were at that awkward moment in the parking lot where the next step is either "I'll call you" or I'm gonna plant one on ya. I did not want to give this guy a chance to do either. I took the initiative and said, "It was nice to meet you. Bye!" Before I knew it, I was in the car and out of the parking lot. I glanced in my rear view mirror and saw him standing there watching me drive off.

Chris - Looking back, I should have given him another chance but.... He was cute, smart and tall and we had a fun conversation. He was definitely a momma's boy and frugal. I paid for my own dinner, which was fine, however he went berserk over how much to leave for a tip. By leaving a $1 bill he would be leaving $.14 cents extra over a 15% tip. He was agonizing for five minutes and eventually left the dollar, although I could tell it killed him inside.

Robert - He was in his early 50's and had never been married. We ordered potato skins and a drink. He took a bite and spit started forming on the corner of his mouth as he was talking to me, the sour cream was frothing and dripped down to his chin. This date lasted 24 minutes.

Richard - He was articulate and funny. We met and he was attractive with a perfect white smile. Even though his sweatshirt was tucked into his jeans I tried to put that in the back of my mind. He ordered a small pizza and I ordered a salad with chicken. After we finished eating he repeatedly gazed my way and when I caught his eye he gave me his sparkling smile. Seeing him look at me that way made me smile right back, bigger and wider each time. As we were leaving we agreed the physical distance between us would be a hindrance to starting a relationship. He obviously couldn't stop looking at me so that was validation enough for me. I got in my car and before I backed out I checked myself in the mirror. There, staring back at me, was a dime sized dark green piece of spinach covering my front teeth.

Tony - We met at a nice Italian restaurant. Early on in the date, I recognized that he clearly was not emotionally over his wife's infidelity. At dinner he carried on about how he wanted to cut his wife's lover's limbs off. In the parking lot, he asked if we could continue dating. I told him I would consider dating once his divorce is final (or once he got out of jail – whichever came first).

My Last Good Date

In the winter of 2002 I ran into John at the cafeteria at work. John and I had known each other for years. We met at our kid's daycare. We made small talk and informed each other of our divorces. I had been single for over five years and it had been two years since his split.

I liked him. I thought he was kind, sweet and had a boyish face. I liked that. As friends, we decided to go to Six Flags without the kids for a fun day. I wasn't sure if it was a date, but I was looking forward to a good time! I wanted to look cute and had a heck of a time picking out an outfit. I settled on a heavy cotton black shirt and a cute pair of shorts with a funky design. When we got to the amusement park, I realized it was hotter than I thought it was going to be. I forgot my sunscreen and just imagined how scorched I was going to get.

The first ride we went on was "Superman", a huge roller coaster with a two hundred and five foot drop. No one in John's immediate circle was interested in going on a roller coaster so he was happy that I was a good sport and agreed to go. As we were standing in line I began to sweat. My face was pretty hot and when I rubbed my forehead it was wet and drippy. John asked me several times if I was okay and I said yes but could only imagine what shade of red my face was at that moment. Soon we were in the seats and were off. I screamed in terror as we plunged down the tracks. As soon as we got off the ride, there were the pictures for sale that captured us mid-plunge. John's picture was almost perfect. He looked calm and had a peaceful half-smile, like he was pushing a baby carriage.

My picture on the other hand: long hair stood straight up, part of my bangs were stuck to my face due to excessive sweating, my mouth was open so wide you could see my tonsils, and my face was as red as a tomato. He asked if he should buy the photo as a memento of our day together. I glared at him, "What do *you* think?"

We had great conversation as we enjoyed several other rides. The temperature was rising by the minute. If only I could stop sweating! John continued to ask me if I was okay, and I assured him I was fine, but I really I wasn't. Basically, I was completely soaked at this point. My underwear was starting to sweat and I felt wet drips streaming down my back. I suggested going on a water ride hoping for some relief. As we settled in on the Raving Rapids and headed toward the first tunnel, we were slammed with the falling water. It felt wonderful even though it was a bit slimy. A few minutes later we went under a waterfall. As we approached, the waterfall was on the opposite side of me, but at the last minute the boat did a complete 180 turn. I was directly under the waterfall. POW! My entire body was pummeled with cool, scummy water. I forgot for a moment that I was on a first date. It felt so refreshing. After the ride I was so drenched that I decided to buy another shirt.

I bought a gray t-shirt with the Six Flags logo on it. I went to the bathroom to change. Oh my. Mascara clumps on my eyelids and black splotches under my eyes. My hair was dripping wet and stuck flat to my face. My underclothes were soaked. I tried to get most of the wetness out of my hair by sticking my head under the dryer. I wiped off my face and was now makeup-free. Even though I looked like a monster from God knows where, physically I felt so much better! After looking at myself I totally expected this to be our first and last date, so I just went with it. I thought "I'm here so I might as well have fun even though I'll never see him again." Too bad, he's a really nice guy.

We continued on our day and had a lot of fun. My underclothes were still wet but I was so much more comfortable. At one point I looked down at my brand new t-shirt and realized that I had two gigantic dark gray wet boob spots. My sopping wet bra had soaked through my new light gray t-shirt. I went into a brain freeze at this point. I folded my hands across my chest for the next twenty minutes and walked a few inches behind him so he couldn't see my embarrassing dark gray circles. The problem for me was I did like him and knew I had blown it.

Later, when he dropped me off at home, I told John that I had a great time and thanked him for dinner. I did not expect to hear from him again, but was happy that I finally had a wonderful first date. I just have to remember to wear an appropriate outfit on my next date.

Happily, I did hear from John again. We were engaged fourteen months later and got married the next year. Later, John told me that he really wanted to come inside after our date but since I just left, he thought I didn't like *him!*

Gayle Suzanne

Granny Rocks!

Part of loving me is having fun. I love a good time. I get the most laughs when I am surrounded by friends. I'm fortunate to have some of the best friends in the world. They bring so much joy to my life.

Another part of loving me is taking care of my physical needs. So why not have an adult product party? I had never even been to one of these parties before and had no idea what to expect. I decided to have ladies night at my house. I had about 18 girls over.

The demonstrator knocked at the door. I was expecting a young girl in her twenties, uninhibited, hip and rough around the edges with tats and piercings all over her face. I opened the door and there stood Mary, a seventy-five-year-old granny. BOING! (Those are my eyeballs popping out of my head). Mary was so mild mannered and sweet. She carried in one plastic bin after another and brought them straight up to my bedroom. Apparently everyone was going to shop from my bed after the demonstration. She wore a polyester shirt with big bold flowers and elastic-waisted pants. Her scent reminded me of my grandmother's mothball closet. She had tight gray curls and was on the pudgy side. This was going to be interesting. Ladies, plenty of drinks in the kitchen!

We all grabbed a seat in the living room anxiously awaiting the start of the show. Mary started off with lotions and nice lingerie-- a little risqué but totally tame. She put a little sample of the lotion on our fingertips and said this particular brand gets hot when applied on skin and induces arousal. The flavors she passed around were peppermint, strawberry and vanilla. She brought out happy penis cream and we all giggled because that was the first naughty word she said. Picturing my grandmother saying that word was cringe worthy… so I took a gulp of my vodka drink.

The most comical part of the night was watching Mary stroke each contraption as she demonstrated them for us. She would turn them on and rub them on the side of her arm and go into great detail about the pleasure spots it would hit. She described each item with a devilish twinkle in her eye. I silently knew that each of us watching her was in a state of shock, although her information was quite educational. Before she explained the actual difference between the two types of orgasms, I thought the only two types were real and fake.

When the demonstration concluded it was time to shop! Mary instructed each of the ladies to wait at the bottom of my staircase. She explained that unfortunately they were not able to *try out* the products before they were purchased. Good to know! She laid out all of the goodies on my bed. All the women were to go in my bedroom one at a time and shop. Everyone picked out their favorites and stuffed them into an anonymous brown paper bag. As each women came down the stairs with her crumbled brown bag the girls downstairs were all over her asking what she bought, practically ripping the bag out of her hand. No anonymity here! Occasionally someone would walk down the stairs and peeking out of the top of the bag was a jumbo penis head. We all took it out and played with it.

I sold over $2,000.00 at that party. I did not realize what a bunch of open minded friends I had (and I'm being subdued with my choice of words here)! As the hostess, I received a cut of the sales in free products, so I was able to enjoy an adventurous shopping spree. I bought one of this and one of that. Those huge, revolving things did not appeal to me, but I thought I would try a cute little silver bullet.

The silver bullet was a smooth, bullet shaped device that had a remote control attached to it. You could switch it from low to high using the clicker. When it was on it made a low pitched buzzing sound. It was very small and discrete looking and was supposed to have the same result as those fancy $350.00 ones. The first time I planned on using it, I wanted to make it a special night. I took a tubby, put on some nice jammies, a little perfume, lit a candle and put on easy listening music in the background. Van Morrison, perhaps? I had never used this type of product before and was quite curious. Plus I thought this was a perfect substitute for a man, because I was not ready for a partner just yet.

My first experience was pretty great and quick. Fast and effective, I could not ask for more. I found a new little buddy that would not hurt me or leave me. Truth be told, I became a little obsessed with my new friend. One night I settled in with my silver mate. I was a pro at this point and buzzed directly from off to high. After a minute or so I smelled something. I turned on the light and the wire attached to my little silver bullet was sparking and smoking.

I killed it.

Gayle Suzanne

Oh Men...Pause

I will confess. I am entering "mid-life" and have accepted the realization that I am no longer a young woman. Soon I will no longer have to purchase feminine products. I'm currently in the 'tween' period, not exactly in the golden years but am beginning to change in many ways.

This is a transitional stage in a woman's life and it is confusing. Things are happening to our minds and bodies that we have no control over. Yep, we might get crabby but it is certainly not our fault... and men, don't question us on that!

So here is a little advice for all you wonderful men out there who have a female loved one who is going through "the change".

OH MEN...PAUSE...IF:

- She walks in the family room with a big smile on her face, goes into the kitchen for a glass of water and returns to the family room sobbing...then walks up the stairs and screams at the cat for looking at her the wrong way.

- She piddles after a sneeze.

- You find your car keys in the freezer.

- You witness in horror her plucking a chin hair in the bathroom.

- She keeps the heat so low you can see your breath as you're watching TV in your living room.

- You want to jokingly refer to her as the tumbleweed.

- She forgets who you are and refers to you by the name of a former boyfriend, or even worse, a former husband.

- You get frustrated with her and want to ask her when her head will start to spin.

- She wakes you up at 3 AM and asks you to help change the sheets that are drenched on her side of the bed.

- She asks you if she looks fat in an outfit. Trust me on this, whatever you think and however irritated you are with her, just say no. No. No. No.

It will be more beneficial for you men to pause, take a breath and remain silent when you want to comment in a negative manner. You will be better off in the long run if you hold your tongue. She will come out on the other side... hopefully... some day.

Friendships

My friends are special treasures. My friends have provided me with many aching jaws, belly aches, and tears from laughter. They have also provided a shoulder to cry on, an ear to listen and a body for me to spoon when we have to sleep in the same bed. I am not jealous of my friends. We are all unique and I love them for who they are. When I informed them I was writing this book, they thought it was going to be about them. That is how much they are a part of my life. I know I could not have gone through life's unpredictable ride without them.

I am proud of the fact that, at one time or another, I have been able to make most of my friends spit out their drink because of the impeccable timing of my jokes.

There have been countless times when my friends and I have been out and people actually have come up to us asking if they could join us. They knew a good time when they saw one! I am so blessed. My friends are strong, independent, intelligent, fun, big-hearted, generous, adventurous, giving, resilient, insightful, spirited, encouraging, inspiring, confident, sincere, loyal, compassionate, beautiful, and kind women. What I find incredible is that we are all drawn together by our similarities and respect each other for our differences. We relate through good times, childhoods, spirituality, challenges, background, kids, school, and life in general.

I would not be who I am today without my incredible group of friends. Each has taught me about loving myself and loving others. I thank them from the bottom of my heart for all they have given me. As I think back to what I endured in eighth grade and look at how blessed I am now, it is a miracle.

PART 4

Going Through Life

Gayle Suzanne

What A Ride

Life is similar to a roller coaster ride. Ups and downs, sharp turns, upset stomachs, blood curdling screams, light headedness, laughter, anticipation, anxiety, hair blowing in the wind, gasping for breath, free falling, relief and the triumph you feel when it is over! Then what do we do? We get right back in line and do it all over again. While in line, we are quiet. Nothing is happening. We are moving a small step at a time, slowly, going through the motions until we are in the middle of another ride.

This past week was a prime example. Over the weekend I had experienced sharp chest pains under my right breast. The pains were so intense they jolted me out of a sound sleep two nights in a row. Two of my aunts had breast cancer so I scheduled a mammogram right away. When I arrived at the office, I was in store for the super duper mammogram. Yeah! My opinion of the three worst doctor appointments are: 1) mammogram 2) dentist; and 3) last but not least, the gynecologist. As I was standing half naked being manipulated for my first 3D x-ray, a wave of anxiety flooded through me. The nurse told me to breathe as she positioned my breast and body in a contorted twisted way. Each time my breast was placed on that cold plastic shelf, it had to be moved ever so slightly. Each time my girls were repositioned it felt like my skin was ripping off. I tried to maintain an upbeat attitude and joked around with the nurse. That's how I cope. For one x-ray shot she knelt down at my feet, raised her hands and manipulated my breast until it was perfectly aligned for the panini press. I peeked down at her and said, "I hope you're buying me dinner after this." I continued on with the jokes asking if we were now exclusive.

After my flattened breasts returned to their natural state, I stopped by my friend's brother's wake. He had recently been diagnosed with a brain tumor and died several weeks later. He was 52 years old. I arrived a few minutes before the doors opened and the line was already halfway down the street. I glanced around and saw dozens of people my age. I imagined they were his classmates, friends or parents of the children he coached for eighteen years. One day he was healthy and vibrant and a few months later, gone from this world. Life is so precious. As I was standing in line, I felt my body go weak and had to literally focus on my breathing to prevent me from collapsing.

After the wake I met my eighty year-old father for dinner. I thoroughly enjoy being with him. He is my rock and so special to me. I just feel love and gratitude when I am around him. Greeting me with his big smile, we settle in as I listen to stories from his younger years. It is such a blessing that he is healthy in mind and body.

The following morning at work I discovered that an email had been forwarded to my superior that questioned my character. Oh great, I should have stayed in bed. I chose to deal with this situation head-on because no one is going to mess with my integrity. I was furious when I read the email. Wisdom told me (and others did too) to take time to calm down before confronting the author of this email. Hours later I made the call. Years ago, this conversation would have made me a giant stress-ball, but I have learned when it is appropriate for me to address an issue and when to let it go. The conversation went well, I received the apology I deserved and steps were made to rectify the situation with my superiors.

The next afternoon I was scheduled for an ultrasound as a follow up to the mammogram to figure out the cause of my stabbing chest pains. I lied still as the x-ray technician squirted goop on my chest and pressed down hard with her smooth instrument. Five minutes later the radiologist peeked in and said "No mass detected." Whew! I think it's time to celebrate with a gooey hot fudge sundae!

That night my daughter, Becca and I went out to dinner. She was heading back to college and I wanted to spend quality time with her. It was bittersweet. We had a great summer and I was sad it was coming to an end. I held back tears knowing how hard it is for me when she leaves. The older she gets, the more I view her as my special friend. She is an amazing young woman.

A few days later my friend Jan and I went to Portsmouth, New Hampshire. We began the day having drinks at this posh restaurant overlooking the ocean. Everyone there was fit and gorgeous. We joked that the couple in front of us had to be models because they both were drop dead gorgeous. She dared me to ask them what they did for a living. So I did. We hit the nail on the head! The gentleman was a model for Calvin Klein and Ralph Lauren Polo. I jokingly questioned if he was an underwear model and he smirked saying, "I don't usually blush, but yes I am." Cool! I gave his stunning companion my business card and asked her to check out my blog. I mentioned that I am a life coach which piqued the gentleman's interest. He told me I had a "light" about me. I have to admit his comment made me feel wonderful inside! A hunky hot male undies MODEL! I felt as giddy as a five-year-old!

The next day was completely uneventful. I got out of bed at noon, caught up on emails, watched a movie, ate dinner and went to bed. It was a relaxing, dull day.

This is how I see it: Fear, laughter, anxiety, joking, silliness, gratitude, sadness, loyalty, letting go, confrontation, confidence, adventure, and then boredom. Life is such an unpredictable experience. We should embrace every day and live life to the fullest. When rough times are upon us, have faith that something joyous will happen soon. It usually does.

To Act Or Not To Act?

When I began to read scriptures from the Bible, I made a commitment to myself to serve others. Shortly afterwards, something miraculous happened. My mind shifted. I felt happier. I started to go outside the parameters of my "bubble life" and connect with others in a way I had never connected before. Out of nowhere my problems did not seem so bad and I felt content.

My idea for reaching out to others was through email, Facebook, text messaging, phone calls, and meeting for lunch. Basically, I used all the normal channels of communication. I did the best I could to keep in touch. Until...

I had been thinking about a coworker whom I worked with for over twelve years. Joan was a poised, classy, wonderful woman. She moved a few hours away after retiring in 2000. When our whole department worked together, we had so many great times. Joan had spouted out hysterical one-liners that have stuck with me to this day. When sharing stories, I like to imitate her with a high pitched squeaky voice. One day, while at work on an Ash Wednesday, it was common to see people walking around with ashes on their foreheads. Seeing this was no big deal, until Roy from another department dropped off a file for Joan.

I heard her way down the hall shouting, "Roy, you have the biggest ashes I've ever seen!"

Of course a few coworkers and I had to check this out. We looked at Roy. It was as if the priest took a paintbrush and swept black tar across his entire forehead. We all shared a great laugh together, Roy included.

One day I walked into her cubicle. She immediately told me to leave as she fanned a folder in front of me. She was shooing me away!

"What's wrong?" I asked with a big smile on my face.

She laughed. "Go away. I just dropped a rose petal!"

That is the most creative, delicate way to describe a toot I have ever heard. Being a brat, I just stood there and teased her. We laughed until we cried.

Joan was involved in a little goof we played on one of the attorneys she worked for. It was during the Anita Hill / Clarence Thomas trial. A bunch of female co-workers and I were we questioning the insanity of the pubic hair and coke can evidence. We came up with this brilliant idea to get a coke can from the vending machine and tape a big clump of head hair on the can and put it on her boss's desk. We had no idea when he would return so we waited patiently for his reaction. Joan was on watch outside his office and gave us the heads up when he got back. A second after he sat down we heard him howl! We all gathered around Joan's desk and busted a gut from laughing so much.

Needless to say we had some great times together. Although we could be a bit distasteful, we had incredibly funny moments and Joan was right in the thick of it. At one point years after she retired, I searched for her on Facebook. I was unsuccessful and thought I would mail her a card to let her know I was thinking of her. I just had this nagging feeling that I should write to her. But I never did send that card. Ironically, I found out later that around the same time I searched for her on Facebook, she passed away.

That was a significant event for me. That little voice inside nudged me to send her a card. Once I learned of her passing, I prayed to God to let her know I was thinking of her and she was a wonderful woman. I cannot continually beat myself up for not sending that card but it did teach me a valuable lesson. Once I get a feeling of reconnecting with someone and letting them know they are thought of, I have to just do it. Not tomorrow, not next week - right now. She was a joy in my life. That was a special time. Thanks for the memories Joan!

Lesson learned.

Game Night

I love playing games. When I was a kid, my family would often play classic board games: Parcheesi, Checkers, Trouble, Go To The Head Of The Class and Battling Tops. We were united and bonded. I am heartfelt when I say those nights were some of my fondest memories as a child. I remember being in my comfy pajamas sitting next to the fire and having so much fun.

As I got older, relatives would visit and we would play cards and dice. My Uncle Joe and Aunt Rosalie would come from Florida and we would stay up late playing games every night. Their game of choice was dice. You had six dice and had to roll a total of 750 points to officially enter the game. My Uncle Joe was such a goofy man. He would get so aggravated and would stand up after every bad roll, walk around his chair a few times and mumble swears in French under his breath. He was the first person I've personally known that had a five hair comb over which started at one ear and ended at the other ear.

When my sister Chris and I wanted to casually introduce a new boyfriend to the family, we would ask him to come over and play cards. It was an easy way for him to get to know our family without any pressure, although at times we got brutal in our game playing. We often played the card game blut. We each would bid on our individual hand, using our best guess of how many hands we could win. If you did not win the exact number of hands you predicted, higher or lower, you would get a blut. The object of the game is NOT to get a blut. But if you happen to get a blut, then it is your job to try to screw everyone else at the table. So you would manipulate the card playing so others would get bluts too! Each blut was worth a nickel so watch out. There was so much screaming and craziness every time we played. One time my brother-in-law got so upset about getting a blut that he reached back and pulled out a bunch of plastic plants from the planter behind him. He did not realize the plants had steel sharp arrows attached to them and if not for our screams, he would have stabbed himself in the head multiple times. Just in time we all yelled, "NOOOOOO!" Can you imagine if he had gone to the emergency room and had to explain that his twenty stab wounds were the result of a $.05 blut?

I have carried over the game night tradition with my family. Every few months or so, we make a night of it starting with a spaghetti and meatball dinner followed by desserts and snacks. Nowadays we play Pictionary, Cranium, Balderdash and other popular games. I know some of my family's most enjoyable times have come from game night.

As simple as it seems, game night can really bring people together in a wonderful, fun, inexpensive, healthy way. Plan one at your home soon!

The Standards I Once Knew Have Left The Building

Every time I watch television, listen to the radio, or observe people, it occurs to me that the standards of decency have slipped.

When watching TV, it's all too common to see a severed head, internal organs, naked butts and listen to curse words and sexual innuendos. I am not a prude by any means, but it does appear that as time goes by we are getting more and more exposed to things that were unthinkable a decade or two ago.

When I was a kid in front of the tube, Rob and Laura slept in separate beds and they were married! If there was a curse word, it was "dang". There was no nudity of any kind and reference to sex was minimal. People did not mention "vajayjays" and we certainly did not see a side boob.

Although I have no control over the standards of the media or what others say and do, I do have control over my own standards. The standards I set for myself are my own personal responsibility. I choose to keep them high.

Here are a few things I'm referring to:

- I will return an item or money if someone in front of me drops it.

- I will not lie to get what I want.

- I will keep a secret.

- I will not use handicapped parking spaces or stalls.

- I will not intentionally cut people off in traffic.

- I will tell the truth if it is in someone's best interest.

- I will not take items home from my employer.

- I will be kind even if I am in a foul mood.

- I will go out of my way for those hurting even if I am exhausted.

- I will not drive while intoxicated.

- I will thoughtfully review my schedule before I commit.

- I will call if I am late for an event or gathering.

- I will dress appropriately.

- I will work hard toward a goal that is important to me.

- I will try to make loved ones feel special and cared for.

- I will go out of my way to help a friend.

- I will speak respectfully.

- I will not enter into a situation unless we both can benefit.

- I will strive for excellence.

- I will be accountable for my actions when I mess up.

- I have a training plan to reach a goal I set for myself.

- I will keep in touch with my family.

- I will follow my intuition and listen to that little voice inside me.

- I will not cheat.

- I will surround myself with loving people.

- I will help and give of myself to the best of my ability.

- I will accept responsibility for the outcome of a situation.

- I will do my best at all times, even when those around me do not.

- I will try to understand a differing opinion.

- I will appreciate the beauty around me.

- I will not take my health for granted.

- I will not engage in malicious gossip.

- I will not steal.

- I will honor others and where they came from.

- I will confront situations head-on only if it is in my best interest and let the rest go.

- I will be sincere.

- I will forgive.

- I will show others how much they mean to me.

This does not mean I don't slip, but when I do, I will not set the bar lower and change these statements to make my life easier. I choose to keep my standards high. It makes life a challenge. I try to live in the narrow path of life.

Space

Most people have their own invisible personal space boundaries. Even though no one goes around drawing a circle around their comfort zone, it is something that is taken for granted. There should be a reasonable amount of space between you and the other person when you are having a conversation, driving, waiting in line, walking through a buffet, or standing in a security line.

We are all familiar with close talkers who sometimes leave a trace of spittle on the side of our face when sharing a story. We move back a few inches, they follow us forward. One time I was at a social work meeting and I was speaking with a vice president from another department. He was a close talker. By the end of the conversation I had backed up from the center of the room to the window. By the time we finished up, my back was up against the blinds and my hair was touching the plastic green plant hanging from the window. I literally had nowhere else to go! Maybe one way to keep the distance between two people is to put your arm straight out in front and tell them, "That's far enough."

My commute is an hour long each way and most of it is on the highway. Why is it that when I'm in the fast lane someone always seems to tailgate me? There is a car in front of me and one to the side of me. Where am I supposed to go? Am I supposed to speed up and jump on the bumper of the car in front of me? Am I supposed to go into the center lane and demolish the person driving to my right? Am I supposed to hit my wing activator and fly away? When I am finally able to change lanes, I need patience in order to forego the nasty glare and finger gesture I want to give as he flies by me (only to tailgate the next person in the way).

When it comes time to get off the highway and go through the tolls, each morning the traffic is backed up. Most days I have to wait because someone in front of me has five car-lengths of empty space in front of them. As I pass by, generally the person driving that car is either texting or on the phone and is not paying any attention to the road in front of him. Because of this, I waste precious time inching my way toward the ramp. As I drive by I see all the empty space - enough space for a plane to land - space that if used up could make my commute that much more pleasant.

Occasionally when I am at a dinner buffet at the salad bar, the lack of boundaries blows my mind. Why do some people stand so close to me? Once I was scooping out mushrooms for my salad (the mushroom container was directly in front of me) and a man behind me in line actually reached his hand over my hand to get beets. Was he in that much of a hurry to get the beets? Why don't people grasp the idea that there should be an invisible three inch boundary between people in a line? It gets really bad when I am waiting in a checkout line at a clothing store and I can feel someone's hot breath on my neck. It's even worse when I can tell that they had a tuna sandwich for lunch. Are they going to checkout more quickly if they stand on the hem of my pants?

This is also true in the airport lines going through security. Several times when I was placing my personal items in the bucket on the conveyor belt, the person next to me pushed their bucket so it touched mine. They did not realize my fingers were on the side of my bucket. It pinched my fingers. It hurt. Why does their bucket have to be so close to my bucket? Why do they have to touch? Can I please have a half inch space between my plastic bucket and yours? Then on the plane – oh boy don't get me started. During a recent flight a woman who boarded the plane before me was applying her lipstick in the aisle and no one could move through. Seriously?

I think there might be a lesson in patience here. Patience for me so I do not get aggravated with things I cannot control - and also patience for those who have to beat me to get to their beets.

Gayle Suzanne

This Six Letter Word Is Worse Than That Four Letter Word

A few years back there was a chunk of time that I'd like to erase from my memory. It was a tough, helpless period of time for me. In November my step-mother, Toni, was admitted to the hospital with severe abdominal pains and constant vomiting. She remained hospitalized for eleven days and was discharged without a solid diagnosis. With the pain and symptoms continuing, the doctors finally detected a growth on her intestines. She was diagnosed with Non-Hodgkins Lymphoma. She had surgery and they were successful in removing it all. She goes twice a year for a PET scan to make sure her cancer is under wraps. Thank goodness she has received encouraging test results!

A month or so later, my sister-in-law, Karen was diagnosed with thyroid cancer. Ugh. Karen is a gem. She is my age and a single mother raising her teenage daughter. She had to go through a surgery to remove the growths plus endure a radioactive iodine treatment where she had to be "quarantined" for two weeks. By the grace of God, Karen is cancer free also.

A few weeks later, my father called me and casually informed me that he had a spot on his lung. He reassured me that it was nothing but he had to have some tests. I hung up with him and immediately called Toni so I could get the real story. She told me the doctors were pretty sure it was malignant.

When you love someone who is sick, you cannot help but feel helpless. We cannot take their pain away or erase their fear of the unknown. My heart went out to my family and I was not sure what I could do. Besides the obvious of calling or sending a card, there really was not much I could do. Just be there for support. I am the type of person who becomes paralyzed hearing bad news. I process at first, listen intently to what the prognosis is and immediately go into how-do-we-fix-this mode. Generally I am able to muster up enough strength to offer support. After the news settles in, I become still, emotionally numb, stare straight ahead in silence with the feelings of shock and disbelief and even denial. As you can imagine during this period, every time the phone rang, my heart would skip a beat.

Sure enough, Daddy had cancer. The nickel-sized tumor was directly in the center of the lower lobe of his lung and the surgeon said the best course of action was to remove the entire lower lobe of his lung. They would have to saw open his ribs and go in through his side to remove the entire tumor properly. I slept over my father's house the night before his surgery so I could be with Toni during the operation. I bought Valentine's Day teddy bears for both of them. Daddy looked at me sweetly, smiled at the bear, rubbed his nose and gently placed him on his pillow. To me, this was such a tender moment. His blue eyes expressed so much to me, even though no words were spoken.

Soon after we arrived at the hospital, Daddy was taken away in his little johnnie. People always look so much smaller in those hideous cotton blue gowns. Thankfully his bum did not peek through-- a visual I did not want to see.

He showed no outward fear. He is a very prideful man. He was totally ready to get this operation over and done with.

Once he was taken away, Toni and I went to the cafeteria for breakfast. She had asked me several weeks earlier to please act calmly in front of him and not flip out, because that reaction would make him nervous. So I decided to flip out hysterically when I was alone and did what she asked. I knew she was very anxious and worried for him also. I was so impressed that she was not letting him see her fear. If she did it would definitely upset him. I witnessed her unconditional love for him and that was pretty amazing. In front of him, she put his feelings before hers. I thought that was beautiful and the true meaning of love.

Seven hours after he went in for surgery, the surgeon came out and said the tumor was successfully removed and he was going to be fine. The tumor, which was the size of a nickel two weeks before, had grown to the size of a small lime. Later, after the biopsy results came back, my father was informed that he had one of the fastest moving cancers. But luckily he was okay. He was okay.

They all were okay.

Having three close family members be diagnosed with cancer around the same time is a pretty dreadful thing to go through. After hearing that everyone was okay, it really put things into perspective for me about not sweating the small stuff. In times like this, the little petty things are not worth getting upset over. We should be thankful each and every day for the blessings in our lives and for the loved ones around us.

Gayle Suzanne

Nope, No Orange Face For Me

Saying goodbye to loved ones who were near and dear is, and always will be, so difficult. Recently, I attended a wake and it made me think about my own services. Even though I will not know what is happening (hopefully) I have a somewhat non-traditional idea of what I would like if I could be at my own funeral.

The whole casket viewing thing is disturbing for me. As I kneel down to pay my respects, I anxiously wait for the closed eyes of the deceased to pop open. Then I'll watch in horror as they sit up in the coffin and lunge at me, trying to grab my throat. Or I will witness their chest rise and fall ever so slightly. Maybe I've watched too many scary movies.

Sometimes, the hairdo on the deceased does not look like her regular hair style. It is flatter or fluffier or matted to the head or parted the wrong way or the bangs are all wrong. It really is a botch job if she looks like one of the Monkeys. Her hair just does not look like it did when I went to lunch with her last month.

Some funeral homes have the potential to do a fabulous job applying makeup, and others not so much. A few deceased I have paid my respects to have actually looked wonderful in the casket. Their coloring was perfect and spot on to what they actually looked like. But I have seen some orange faces that were pretty disturbing. His face was definitely not orange yesterday.

It is emotionally challenging to see someone I love, motionless and even worse, not looking like the person I knew and treasured. I want to remember them in my mind as they were at their healthiest.

I also want that for myself.

I recently made a list of instructions for my own funeral arrangements. These are my own personal wishes and not intended to offend anyone. I would like to forego a traditional wake and instead have a fun celebration of my life with fine food, uplifting music and succulent desserts, including plenty of chocolate!

I think Ave Maria is one of the most gorgeous songs ever, but I do not want it playing at my funeral. I would like songs from my iPod to be blasting in the room. A little Owl City, Journey, Loverboy, Pat Benatar, Lady Gaga, James Durbin, Elvis, Bruce Springsteen, Garth Brooks. I would like only top ten hits and dance music.

I'd like to be cremated. Someone please bring my ashes in a box or a bowl and everyone can take a spoonful of me home if they so choose (my love ones think this is gross. My response: "Don't you want a piece of me?"). I would enjoy a roomful of happy pictures but please select the ones with minimal chins. There will be a microphone in the room and each person will have the opportunity to tell a goofy story. I want it to be a celebration of my life, not a sad time. I have strong faith that when my time comes I will go to a wonderful place. I will make sure that when I go to that wonderful place, I will request the option of looking after all of the people I left behind.

It's Only A Number

Even though I'm approaching-- ahem-- age fifty, I still feel as young and crazy as I did in college. I've been close with my college friends for over thirty years. We make it a point to get together every other month or so. When we are together we revert back to being giddy teenagers.

Last year I took a trip to Florida with my old roommate. Her parents' condo happened to be right up the street from a famous teen heartthrob. What would a mature almost fifty-year-old woman do in this situation? You got it. We belted out *I Think I Love You* outside his house at 2 AM. Disappointingly, he did not come outside and greet us. So the next day we went back to his gated home and my friend (who I might add is *older* than me but not quite as mature) proceeded to dig through his garbage to find a souvenir for us to take home. Her search was cut short when a police car rounded the corner. She had precisely three seconds to bolt back to the car and shift into gear. I did not witness the whole scene as I was scrunched down beneath the dashboard. I have my pride.

As I think back, I recall how our conversations have evolved over the years:

During College:

"Did you scoop anyone this weekend?"

"Can I borrow some money, I only have a roll of nickels for the week."

"Want to split the cost of a jug of wine?"

"Who wants to go to Ft. Lauderdale for spring break?"

"I don't have a clue what I want to do for the rest of my life!"

"I have to take baby math senior year in order to graduate. Ugh!"

"I am going to be up all night studying. Better stock up on chocolate."

"Have you done it with him yet?"

"Who will be the first to get married?"

"Can I borrow your crock pot?"

Twenties:

"I was invited to eight weddings this summer and I'm in five of them!"

"Oh, you can definitely wear this bridesmaid's dress for other events!"

"I can't believe you're pregnant!"

"Your next whoopee assignment with your husband is..."

"Working forty hours a week is exhausting, I miss college."

"After paying rent, heat, electricity, I have ten dollars left for the month."

"I'm cooking my first turkey, what do I do with the gizzards?"

"When are you going to move out of your parent's house?"

"I cannot believe you guys are playing strip poker in the kitchen on a school night!

"I have a job interview tomorrow!"

"What's a 401K?"

Thirties:

"I'm so sorry about your divorce."

"What do you get someone for their second wedding? They already have nice towels."

"My baby is starting first grade!"

"I'm not going to drink much tonight, it takes me three days to get over a hangover."

"We just got a puppy."

Whispering: "When you guys are intimate with your husband, have you ever queefed?"

"I have to start dying my hair, I'm loaded with gray."

"I think I might go back to school to get my masters."

"Look at these lines under my eyes!"

"I cannot lose this baby weight and it's been 8 years since I gave birth!"

"Would you ever consider having plastic surgery or botox?"

"Do any of you pee a little when you sneeze?"

"We finally paid off our student loans!"

"Paying for daycare and the mortgage is brutal."

Forties:

"I'm so hot!"

"I'm going to wear flat, comfortable shoes and I don't care."

"Everything is sagging!"

"I can't believe how much college tuition is!"

"What? I can't hear you!"

"I cannot read this label."

"I chopped off my hair."

"How should I talk to my teenager about sex? Ugh."

"I really do not want to take my sixteen-year-old out driving anymore, last time she almost wiped out a mailbox."

"It's time to trim the hair in your ears."

"I received my first Botox treatment! No more crinkle in my forehead!" "Do any of you pee a little when you laugh?"

"My back hurts."

"I'm so sorry for the loss of your mother."

"What did you say?"

As I look closely around me, there are women who have aged beautifully and look awesome and can still hear, so that is encouraging! My sister Chris, and my sister-in-laws, Maryellen, Karen and Robin are the perfect examples. They are lovely, fit, wrinkle-free, vibrant, youthful and dress beautifully. There is hope!

Gayle Suzanne

Off To School We Go

Thinking about Becca leaving for college has made my mind drift to the past. I have been sifting through many memories when she was a little girl. When I think about her making up her new bed in the college dorm, my mind shifts to when she was three and ready for a twin bed. It was a challenge because in order for her to move up the ranks we had to wean her off the binky...or should I say *binkies*. Her routine was to sleep with six of them. One in her mouth bobbing up and down like crazy – two more with her tiny pinky fingers stuck in the holes on each side of the binkies (she would jab the rubbery part in the corners of her eyes), two more held by her thumb and pointing finger that she would tap on her cheeks, and the last binky stashed under her pillow just in case one fell onto the floor. Every night I would check on her and the binkies would be stuck all over her face – forehead, cheeks, and the one in her mouth moving at full speed.

We did eventually wean her off the pacifiers – well, she made the decision herself. Parenting tip: We would cut a small hole in each of the pacifiers one by one. When she started sucking on them she would toss them out of her crib yelling, "This one doesn't work!" It took a month or so to get rid of the three hundred binkies that we had lying around the car, the house, the diaper bag, the sofa, the glove compartment, the pocketbook, the lunch box the stash in her room, the crib, the bathtub, the laundry bucket, the kitchen drawers and jacket pockets. When we were down to the last one, I told her if she threw it away we will not buy another one AND once they were all gone, a nice new *big girl* bed would be waiting for her! A couple of restless nights and she tossed her last binky away.

Success!

...Until she realized she was not caged in anymore and could get up whenever she wanted.

On her first day of elementary school, all the neighborhood kids and parents stood at the bus stop and took pictures of the kids on their special day! Becca had a purple fleece jacket on and a sticker shaped like a pencil saying Room 12 Mrs. Frankel. Her backpack was sparkling clean on that first day (unlike the last day of school when it was filthy). She wore a pair of Dora The Explorer sandals with blue toenail and finger polish. She was so excited to start school! As the bus arrived I gave her a big hug and kiss goodbye and told her to have a wonderful day! Still waiving to her, I got in my car and watched the bus drive away. I turned and signaled right as the bus signaled left. I was trying to detach from the hardest day of motherhood so far – but as a few tears fell on my cheek, I turned around and followed the bus to school. I stayed back a bit because I did not want her to catch me stalking her on that first day. I sneakily drove into the parking lot and went as far as I was allowed. I watched her get off the bus with a neighborhood friend and enter the big brick building. She seemed fine on her new adventure. It took me a while to stop following the bus every day. Maybe it was because I was late for work that entire week.

Now that she's all grown up, I yearn for time to stand still. In my eyes she will always be my precious, little girl. But this is her time and she will flourish. I have to let her go. I have faith that she will always remain close.

Rare Moment

I guess I would consider myself a fairly average looking woman. I am no beauty queen, but I consistently try to put myself together the best I can. My appearance has never been the envy of other women. I am perfectly fine with that. However, there was an incident in my life when I had a glimpse of what that would be like.

Rewind to when I was a freshman in college. I lived on an all girl floor with about seventy first year students. Over time, I became friendly with most of the girls even though only a handful would hang out in our room. The most girls we had in our room at one time were probably five, and that was to watch The Thornbirds on TV. ("No More Ralph, No More!) I had a few male friends visit during the year but it was not a frequent event.

Because I was on a college budget, I had to find a way to make some extra cash. Every now and then when my bangs would twirl wildly with cowlicks, I would trim them myself rather than spend my sacred pub money. I would hold a clump of hair out in front of me and snip-- pretty easy. After witnessing my classic haircutting style, my roommates began requesting a trim. Eventually I was giving full blown haircuts. I really did not have a clue what I was doing but they seemed pleased with the results and the cost savings. No one ever stepped out of my room looking like Jim Carey from Dumb and Dumber, so all was good. Later that first semester I got a real client, a junior who would come to my room every month. He paid me three dollars, my going rate. Other than that I would do a trim here and there for the girls on my floor. I actually made enough cash to partake in weekend social outings.

As a freshman I went to parties that only allowed freshmen. We had to work our way up to an upperclassman party or know someone who knew someone. I was aware of the big names on campus, but never spoke with them. Conveniently my adorable roommate was seeing a football player and he invited her and her friends to a football party. There would be upperclassmen there, which was the ultimate in cool. I was going to be cool.

At some point during the party I was approached by one the Keener twins (name changed to protect the insane hotness of these twins). The Keener twins were basically the Brad and Bart Pitt of my small Catholic college. Seriously to die for gorgeous, unattainable, GQ material. I could not imagine why he would want to talk with me. My mind wandered. Does he want me to refill the potato chip bowl? Does he want me to steal some toilet paper from the student center? Does he want me to get him a beer?

As he stood in front of me, he smiled, "Hi Gayle. I hear you cut hair. Would you be able to cut mine?"

The word was out-- even to senior hunks!

Luckily I had a few drinks in me and was able to mutter, "Sure. Come to room 332 at noon tomorrow."

"Okay. Great. Thanks!"

I think I blacked out at that point.

The next day starting at 11:55 AM, I anxiously waited to see if he would show up. For a moment, I questioned if I was actually conscious when we had that conversation. My dormitory floor was shaped like an "L" and my room was at the end of the longest hallway. It was noon and he was right on time. He walked down the hall like a normal person, but to me he was strutting down the runway in a fashion show. Girls were fluttering around doing a double take as he was walking down the hall toward *someone's* room. I knew each of the girls was wondering where the heck he was going! What was this hunky, gorgeous, movie star-like SENIOR doing on a freshman girls restricted floor on a Sunday afternoon? I greeted him and glanced down the hall at a dozen girls watching as he turned into *my* room. I wonder what they thought about that!

He was pleasant and gracious. I must have had a shot of something before he arrived because I was quite charming myself. I gave him my towel and asked him to wet his hair in the girl's shower. I was very glad that my towel was downy fresh and not stinky moldy. He sat down in the middle of my miniscule triple and I combed through his hair slowly. Over the next half hour about twenty girls stopped by for a visit. Girls I did not even know were popping their heads in my room asking to borrow a paper clip or piece of tape. I knew they were just being nosy but I did not care because he was in *my* room.

At that rare moment I felt a glimpse of what it would feel like to be the envy of all... and honestly, I think I was!

PART 5

Serving Others

The Grocery Store Experiment

I bet you can think back to specific times in your life when someone touched your heart. It probably didn't take much-- a smile, a note, a kind word, a moment of encouragement. Sometimes an insignificant gesture can move someone through a dark place to a place of hope. I remember kind words, sweet deeds and simple smiles which helped shift my attitude and in turn felt so good. When you think about people who have gone out of their way for you, I'm sure you smile and think good thoughts. If you are that person who goes out of your way for others, they will want to be around you. When you help, encourage, lift others up and shine, people will gravitate towards you and want to be around you. When you give love, you get love.

Try the Grocery Store Smile experiment. As you enter the store, commit to smile at as many people as possible. As you're pushing your cart around, look random people in the eyes and smile. Guaranteed, most if not all, will smile back. Do this from the cottage cheese to the deli to the bakery to the register to the parking lot. Pay attention to how you feel as your smile is reciprocated. See what your mood is when you get in your car to return home. It's an amazing experience-- one you can do without spending a dime.

As life passes by, make an effort to encourage someone, smile at a stranger, give a sincere compliment or lift someone's spirits. Be a bright light and shine around them! It sounds easy, right? Yet, do we take advantage of opportunities to act on these simple gestures? Do we make that extra effort to actually tell someone we like her scarf?

Looking back at my younger school years, I wish more people had smiled at me, sat with me at lunch or said something nice to me. I wish that popular teenager in the mainstream would have thought "Nope, I'm not going to pick on her today, I'm going to just smile at her."

Mealin On Wheelin

For some time, I have wanted to volunteer for something hands on. A friend of mine mentioned that she delivers meals once a week and they needed help in my town. I called the director of volunteers, had an interview and was hired to deliver the meals. Interestingly enough, the director said she put an ad in the paper seeking someone in my town and no one answered. Then a few weeks later she received my random phone call. She told me that hearing from me was her answer from God. My intention starting Meals on Wheels was thinking that I could help some elderly people. The funny thing is after a year of wheelin I think I'm the one who is really benefiting from it.

It took me a few weeks to get the route down. Luckily Becca and her friend tagged along with me on my first day solo. Goodness knows how many doors I knocked on only to realize it was the wrong house! Other times I have heard, "I'm in the bathroom!" Most of the older men call me honey and sweetie and dear. One of the men looks just like my father. He is adorable! It warms my heart delivering to him! Sometimes elderly women greet me at the door in their snugly pink bathrobes with matching slippers. Sometimes they'll meet me at the door in their long johns. I have been greeted by chickens, cows and goats. I've been asked to come in and look at beautiful handmade quilts, crocheted sweaters, handmade dolls and one elderly woman took my hand and escorted me into her bathroom so I could see her new tub with fancy jets. The best part about that tub is that it really gets in between her toes! I serve the oldest woman in our town who is a special ninety-seven-year-old treasure!

One day Jean said to me. "How would we eat if you didn't come by?"

Since I was a little kid I have had a desire to help other people. I think having a rough time when I was younger made me appreciate kindness from others. That probably was the greatest gift that came out of my bullying days.

For some reason throughout my life, I had a belief that I could only do something worthwhile if I had a billion dollars. If I did, then I could really make a difference and build a school, a well, an apartment building or send a bunch of people to college, or build an orphanage. Seeing that I am not able to do any of those things, I felt the little things I actually could do really did not mean that much.

One of the sweetest women I deliver to is eighty-four-years-old and her name is Lanie. Her speech is slurred and she does not have full use of her hands. Because of this, I was asked to set up her food when I delivered. Each time I arrived to her home, she had the table neatly set up with a clean placemat, silverware, napkin and an empty cup. I poured her milk into the cup, buttered her bread and removed the cellophane off of her hot meal.

One day I was later than usual due to a winter storm and treacherous roads. I came in the door and apologized for being late. Lanie was standing in the kitchen rummaging through a loaf of bread. I could tell she was very hungry. I noticed bananas on the table and asked her if she wanted me to peel one for her before I prepared her lunch.

"Yes! Thank you, Thank you! I'm so hungry!"

I peeled the banana and handed it to her. She gobbled it down in a very short time. She was so happy to be eating something. At that moment, Lanie's gratitude made me lose my breath. That incident helped me realize that peeling a banana meant something bigger to Lanie than it did to me. To her, it was the difference between being hungry and not being hungry. To me, it was nothing.

Don't underestimate the impact of something small that you do for someone else. Do not let the fact that you think it is small stop you from doing it. Something to you that seems insignificant could change someone's life. It could help them for that moment or for the rest of their lives. You never know.

I am a deep believer that our happiness is directly related to doing and acknowledging the little things in life. When doing seemingly insignificant things for others becomes a part of your life, do not be surprised if your life changes for the better. I am a firm believer that you reap what you sow. Keep on doing the little things and watch your life flourish in countless ways.

Gayle Suzanne

Women Need Support Too!

Each year for Christmas my sister, Chris, buys her daughter an assortment of underwear and bras. One Christmas my niece opened up a large box which was filled with men's flannel shirts and socks. She holds up the socks and confusingly asked, "Mom, what are these?" Somewhere across town Chris's ex-husband unwrapped a gift filled with bras and panties from his ex-wife.

I bet each woman reading this has a few bras in her drawer that are taking up space with no intention to be worn ever again. I'm sure those bras have not held up anything in years. And there are those bras that you should never, ever wear. We all know the ones...

- The bra that's too small and cuts off right in the middle of your boobs, so when you wear it with a tight sweater it looks like you have 4 boobs.

- You wear that same bra and the extra boobs are popping out of your back.

- The bra that you can barely clasp but one day you believe you'll finally fit into... even though it's been ten years since you've seen it. Just like those size 6 jeans in your closet.

- The bra straps that leave a one inch laceration in your shoulders.

- The sexy bra that your husband or lover is so excited to see you in and you have no desire to wear – the thought of the girls being squashed so tightly... and cleavage up to your chin.....ugh

- The sports bra that miraculously turns two boobs into a uniboob.

- The annoying bra with loose straps that you have to constantly pull up.

- The bra that is held together by a safety pin or a paper clip.

- The maternity bra that you wore when you were pregnant or nursing. I know mine was so huge that I could have strung the straps to a tree and used it as a hammock for Becca.

- The stiff, lacey bra-- just the thought of putting it on makes you want to scratch your eyeballs out.

- The bra where the end of the underwire pokes through your skin and gives you a puncture wound requiring stitches.

- For those of you with small ones, the water bras. Only heard of them... can't even imagine.

- The bras that have 18 hooks that you just don't have enough time to put on before work and requires four people to take off.

- The super tight bra that makes you look awesome but when you take it off every inch of your chest screams for air.

- The bra that you wear that does not do anything – your puppies are in the same place they would have been had you worn nothing at all.

There are some things in life that we take for granted. When my bras fall into one of the categories above, I don't think twice about replacing them. Others are not so lucky. In tough times, a woman will choose food and heat **for her children over a bra** for herself. The Bra Recylers is a non-profit organization that recycles *gently used, clean bras* to women in need all over the world.

Take a few minutes, clean out your bra drawer, get a small box, put a few stamps on it and make a difference in a woman's life! So easy. Maybe a bra that looks and feels awful on you will be the perfect fit for someone else!

www.brarecycling.com

Gayle Suzanne

Toss Judgment Aside

Recently my husband and I visited my stepson in Kentucky. One of our little side trips was to a nearby Barnes and Noble. After poking around for about 20 minutes, I heard a screech from the back of the store. It was a high pitched scream from a child and echoed throughout the store. My first reaction was this was a child being tortured, but then realistically thought he was just misbehaving. I shook my head for a split second thinking he should be removed. After all, a book store should be quiet and peaceful.

A minute later out of the corner of my eye I saw a woman pushing a baby carriage and counting, "1, 2, 3 Okay we're leaving."

I heard another howl that was bigger than the last. She went over to her three-year-old, scooped him up and left the store. I watched as she pushed through the first set of doors and remained in the entrance way. Her son wet-noodled out of her arms and slid to the floor as he screamed bloody murder.

As I was witnessing this temper tantrum, I thought back to when Becca was three years old. We were at a drug store a few days before Easter. On the bottom shelf Becca spotted a huge stuffed blue Easter Bunny. She grabbed it and hugged it. Happily she exclaimed, "Beader Bunny, Beader Bunny. I want this Beader Bunny!"

After I told her no (because of course I already had a beader bunny stashed away in the hall closet) she and the oversized big bunny ran away from me screaming. Like a good mother, I chased her. Checking each aisle, I got a quick glimpse of her and off she went. After a few minutes of this I loudly said I was going to leave on three. 1, 2... I caught her! Unfortunately for me, we were nowhere near the exit. I had to walk through the entire length of the store with her kicking and thrashing about. One only knows how many disapproving glances came my way. All I know is I did the best I could at that moment.

I looked back at the entrance and saw the look of exhaustion on that mother's face. I decided to put all judgment aside and see if she needed a hand. I was not sure if she would be offended by my asking to help, but thinking back, it would have been nice if someone helped me during the blue bunny fiasco. I pushed open the glass doors and asked if could do anything to help her. I saw her eyes shift as if to say thank goodness.

"Yes, if you would please push the stroller while I carry my son to my car. He really needs to settle down."

I gladly obliged. I peeked in the carriage to see an adorable six-month-old little boy who was quiet as a mouse. Her three-year-old finally settled a bit. He kept turning around looking at me, probably thinking "Who the heck is that?" When we arrived at her car, she gently placed the three-year-old inside and rolled down the windows.

He wailed and tried to climb out, first out of the front window, then out the back. I told her to watch the baby and I would put her oldest in the car seat. Eventually he would stop screaming. After I safely secured him she began to sob. She told me she tried to do the right thing and leave the store. Her husband was deployed and she was alone caring for her children. I rubbed her back and asked her to take a breath and relax for a few minutes. Her children were safe and she needed a moment to herself.

She calmed down, hugged me and thanked me. I was gone about fifteen minutes and thought that my husband and stepson probably might be wondering where I was. I left my cell phone in the car (as usual) so I couldn't call them. As soon as I re-entered the store I saw both of them searching down the aisles. I called out to my husband.

He turned around and calmly said, "I was ready to call the police." I rationalized and said I could have been in the bathroom, but he admitted he checked there too.

If you're out and about and notice someone in distress, rather than judging, reach out and help instead.

Gayle Suzanne

Ways To Serve

Things to do for others in 1 - 60 seconds:

- Turn off your high beams if you are driving behind someone at night.

- Use your blinker for all turns.

- Take a few seconds and breathe before you say something hurtful or something you'll regret.

- Ask God to make you a vessel of love and bring someone in your life you can help.

- Smile and say "Good morning!" to someone at work or in a store.

- Hit your brakes if you are tailgating someone-- remember how irritating it is when someone tailgates you especially when there is nowhere for you to go

- Rub someone's back as you walk by them. A gentle touch can make someone feel so good!

- Hold the door open for someone who is walking behind you.

- If someone drops something in front of you, let them know or pick it up for them.

- Look someone in the eye and say I'm sorry and mean it.

- Tell a special person you love them.

- When you sit down in church, acknowledge and smile at the people you are sitting next to.

- Pray to God to bless those you love.

- Buy a treat for a child in the grocery store line (but ask permission first).

- Tell someone about a great show or book or movie that they would enjoy. Tell them you were thinking of them.

- Call for your pet to sit on your lap and pet him.

- If someone is short a little bit of money at a store, offer to give it to them without them paying you back.

- If you see someone walking on the side of the road and there are puddles everywhere, drive away from them as you are passing them so they don't get hit with a wave of water.

- In any situation-- work, home, social-- give credit where credit is due.

- If someone lets you go ahead of them in the car, wave to them as a thank you and acknowledgment.

- Even if you're in a bad mood, greet others with a smile and happy demeanor.

- Say please and thank you.

- If you're wearing a hat to an event, remove it before you sit down.

- When you're talking with someone on the phone and someone asks you something, take the phone away from your ear for a few seconds to answer politely.

- Compliment your children more than you criticize them. Lift them up and encourage them and be proud of their accomplishments. Say "good job!" when they try, even though it might not be perfect.

- If you're not handicapped, don't park in the handicapped spot.

- Pay for someone's toll who is behind you If it is $1.00 toll for everyone, pay for the next car or two behind you.

- Think about the service your waitress/waiter gave you and give a generous tip.

- When speaking with several people, have eye contact with everyone.

- Forgive someone who did you wrong.

- Go out of your way to be extra friendly to a frazzled clerk.

- Let someone else have the parking space you're both aiming to get. Take the next available space. The extra minute of walking will be good exercise .

- Hug someone a bit longer than usual.

- Compliment someone every day. "Your outfit is beautiful." "Your hair looks nice." "I like your necklace." "You're such a hard worker." "That's a pretty sweater." "You have a nice smile." "Your eyes are gorgeous."

- Look into your child's eyes and tell them you are proud of them just for who they are.

- If you can't keep a commitment, as a courtesy, let the host know so they can plan accordingly. Do not pull a no show.

- When being turned down for a date, brush yourself off and move on. Don't take it personally. That just wasn't the right person for you.

- Return your shopping cart to the designated area.

- Play a game so you can remember someone's name. It always makes you feel nice when someone remembers who you are.

- Choose to not respond to crabby, negative people you randomly meet.

- Send an email to a friend who is going through a hard time.

- Go out of your way to encourage someone and build them up.

- If you see someone who has a brake light out or a headlight out, let them know.

- Let someone go before you in line. If they have less articles than you or if they are returning a movie to a Redbox and you are searching for one, by all means let them go first.

- Really listen to someone when they are telling you about something. Don't interrupt or anxiously wait to talk about yourself. Just listen and be attentive. Ask questions about them.

- When in line at a coffee shop, offer to buy someone a cup of coffee or tea.

- If you're in line behind a parent with his/her irritable young child-- play peek a boo a couple of times with the child. It might distract him and save the parent from anxiety.

- If someone working at your doctor's office is repeatedly rude to you, let the office manager know. This is a reflection of the owner and I'm sure he would appreciate knowing that the staff is rude.

- If someone is stranded on the side of the road, roll down your window and ask if they need you to call someone for them.

- If someone is walking around with something embarrassing hanging out, let them know gently.

- If you see someone in a parking lot who is struggling with a package, go over and offer to help.

- If a coworker wears a cast, offer to carry their lunch or get their lunch for them.

- If someone you love places third instead of first, tell them how proud you are of them!

- If you see someone waiting to cross the street (especially in bad weather), let them cross even if you have a green light. You are in a nice warm car and they might be freezing or drenched.

Things to do for others in 1 - 5 minutes:

- Enjoy a sunset with a loved one.

- Write a card to someone who is sad and hurting just to let them know you are thinking about them.

- Leave a few minutes early so you are not late for an event.

- Think of someone you can fix a friend up with. Take a risk and ask both parties if they would be interested in meeting one another.

- Bring a small gift to someone you are visiting.

- If you know someone who is sick, call them and ask them if you can help with anything.

- If someone compliments a piece of jewelry or an article of clothing that you are wearing, take it off and give it to them.

- If you are in a store and items are 75% off that would make good gifts, pick up a few at discounted prices and keep them on hand when you need a gift for someone.

- Write out a little post it note in your child's lunch or your spouse's briefcase-- just to say I love you!

- If someone goes out of their comfort zone and tries something new, tell them how proud you are for their courage and that you realize that must have been so difficult for them to do!

- Think before you tell someone they are wrong. If their idea is different from yours it might just be different, not necessarily wrong. There might be more than one way to handle a situation and if it's different from yours and it works for them, don't say anything. Just accept it.

- Listen to a favorite song-- one that inspires, or one that makes you want to dance, or one that makes you think of someone special

- Share something you love with others. If you like to read, tell them about a great book. If you like to woodwork, show them a beautiful piece you made-- you might inspire someone else.

- If someone is searching for a book in a bookstore and you are nearby with a favorite book, let them know it was a great one.

- If you ding a car next to you accidentally, leave a note with your contact information.

- Write a personal note or a funny story about your relationship in someone's birthday card.

- If you see things have fallen on the floor in a

department store, pick it up and hang it up instead of walking over it.

Things to do for others in 5 - 15 minutes:

- Before checking out of a hotel room, put all trash away in the baskets and put all towels in a pile rather scattered all over the room.

- Walk along a beach and breathe deeply.

- If you're having a lonely day, pick up the phone and call someone else who might be lonely. It will make them feel special and neither one of you will be lonely.

- Tell the truth.

- Think of someone who has no plans for the holidays and call them and invite them to join you and your other guests.

- When wiping snow off your car, wipe off the snow on the car next to you.

- Buy someone a gift without expecting one in return.

- Purchase a few $1 or $5 gift cards from Dunkin Donuts or McDonalds and give them out to people who stand on corners asking for help. This way they are sure to get a coffee and sandwich if they are hungry. Keep these in your car or wallet so they are at your disposal to help someone out.

- Enjoy a nice cup of tea.

- Go through your calendar and write in birthdays or special dates you don't want to forget.

- If you have a family member or friend who has lost a spouse or a parent, call them after the services and keep in touch. So many people I've known who've lost someone have had a hard time a few weeks after the services when all is quiet. Think of them during holidays because this is a hard time of year for them. If a child has lost a parent, send them a special card on Father's Day or Mother's Day. We tend to live our lives but others are struggling so much and a little card or phone call can make a huge impact.

- Take time to tell the important people in your life that they are important.

- If you are making yourself lunch or dinner, ask family members if they want something also   .

- Register for a class and ask a friend to join you.

Things to do for others in 15 minutes or more:

- Burn a CD of your favorite uplifting songs and give it to a friend.

- Have a social gathering at your house for your friends and invite single friends of both sexes.

- Clean out a part of a closet/ cellar/ attic once a month and give away something you don't use.

- Take a long hot bath and lotion your skin with nice smelling products.

- If you like to knit, sew, bake, or garden, find a charity where you can donate items to.

- Pick some flowers from your garden or from a field and give them to a neighbor or friend or put them in a favorite spot in your home.

- If you know someone who is ill, offer to clean their house, do laundry, pick up a prescription for them or offer to do their grocery shopping.

- If you are single, buy yourself a gift or two in August, wrap them up and put them under the tree for yourself for Christmas. It doesn't have to be expensive, just something that you love.

- Make a batch of cookies and give them to someone who is going through a tough time.

- Look through a craft book and make a few little trinkets. Keep them in your car or home and randomly give them to folks who need a little pick me up.

- If a friend's loved one dies, acknowledge it by attending the wake or funeral if you can. No one likes to go to those functions, but you go to show support for the ones left behind.

PART 6

Just For Fun

Still Got It

My husband, John, and I like to go to concerts. We enjoy various types of music and one of his favorite bands is Coldplay. They were performing nearby and we planned to make a little weekend of it. At the time, we were both in our forties.

I'm grateful that he has a variety of interests including concerts, plays, hiking, and going to museums. It's something we have in common and I believe doing different things keeps us young and with it.

The concert was on a Friday night and we had checked into our room early. We had a little nap before it was time to rock out. As we sat in the arena, we were looking around and I joked with John saying he was the oldest person in the arena. There were twenty-year-olds everywhere.

He glanced around the floor and said, "Nope, that guy is older than me!"

Yeah, he was right. Over the next few minutes we saw a handful of people who were probably in their fifties, so yes, older than John. He appeared to fluff it off but I think he was a little offended, so I looked at him, grabbed his hand and said, "Oh honey, we're still cool for doing this at our age. I mean, we still got it, right? We're pretty hip for being here with all these young people." He smiled and all was good.

The warm up band came on and we rose to our feet. The entire stadium started clapping. We joined along and knew we were in for an awesome night. The lights were still on full tilt and we felt the heightened energy of the room. I looked over at John and he was grinning ear to ear. I felt youthful and free! Out of the corner of my eye, I noticed something white sticking out of his sleeve. I pulled on it. It was a dryer sheet.

Well, at least I've still got it.

Quirky Jobs

I've gained so much insight from my crazy jobs. I learned life lessons along the way. Have a laugh at my expense, it's all good.

My first job was at a local coffee shop when I was a freshman in high school. This is where I learned the ten second rule about food. Once in a while, the cook would drop a piece of bacon or toast on the floor. He would quickly pick it up, blow on it, and put it back on the plate for me to serve. I was so young I didn't realize the magnitude of how gross that was. I want to apologize to all the customers out there who were served a blown-on, fallen sausage.

During college, I was a part time manager in the deli/snack shop on campus. One of my Sunday night responsibilities was to prepare a huge vat of tuna salad for the Monday lunch rush. The recipe called for pimentos. I don't like pimentos, so I made the executive decision not to add them to the tuna salad. One day the lunch lady working the Monday morning shift pulled me aside and questioned my executive decision.

"Gayle, why aren't there any pimentos in the tuna salad? For months we've been ordering cans of pimentos because we thought we were out of stock!"

I smugly replied, "I don't like pimentos. I really don't think there should be any red things in tuna salad."

She took my hand and lead me to the supply closet and pointed to forty industrial sized cans of pimentos on the bottom shelf. Oops.

The summer of my freshman year in college my brother-in-law, Frank, hired me to drive a ding dong cart (a.k.a. ice cream truck) three days a week. Frank drove the other four days. What a cool way to spend the summer at age seventeen! Truth be told, I made gobs and gobs of money! Who would have thought that handing out ice cream and ringing an annoying bell all day long would be so lucrative!

Although the truck was filled with freezers for the ice cream, the actual vehicle did not have air conditioning. On a 100 degree day, I would be driving at the zippy speed of five mph with the sun beating down on me. Each time I saw a little kid run out of his house, I had to stick my head in a twenty degree freezer and retrieve a Mickey Mouse bar for him. Most days by noontime, I had a massive headache. The route required a daily stop at a town pool. To get to the pool area, I had to carefully maneuver the truck through a narrow gate. Driving into the area, it literally left two inches of space on either side to get through without incident. The dirt road was full of holes so I had to white knuckle it and pull in perfectly straight. As I drove through the gate one afternoon, I heard a sound louder and worse than a chalkboard scratch. Bolting out of the truck I examined the ten foot long scratch, multiple dents, and a smashed window. The pictures of the rocket bars and strawberry shortcakes were distorted and unrecognizable. Ugh! Thankfully Frank and my sister were compassionate and understanding. Thanks guys!

One week when my sister and Frank went on vacation, he asked me to work the seven days they would be away. You probably wouldn't guess it, but one can become a bit delirious when working seven ten-hour days in the hot sun ringing a damn ice cream bell. At the end of the seventh day as I was heading home, I noticed a kid run from his house to the street. I pulled over and waited. I was tired and getting aggravated wondering why this kid was taking so long to come over and get his ice cream. Then I realized I was sitting in my Altima.

MY WORST JOB EVER. My step-mother's brother, John, went out of his way to get me this job. It was in 1985 and jobs were scarce. Hourly Rate: $3.80 which was $.05 more than minimum wage. This job was at a factory which manufactured perfume, glass cleaner, shampoo, conditioner, ant traps, bleach and shaving cream.

They hired about twenty college students and our job was to stand at an assembly line and perform the menial tasks assigned. On the perfume line, we would take small black tops and place them over the opening of the bottles. The perfume bottles flew through the conveyor belt so quickly that we had to be alert. It was like the I Love Lucy episode where Lucy and Ethel worked at the chocolate factory. Problem was we couldn't shove the perfume bottles in our aprons or our mouths. There was no place to hide the stinky perfume if you missed one.

I actually enjoyed the ant trap line because we could sit down. All other lines had to be performed while standing. Most tasks required us to place caps on the top of bottles or stick the squirt sticks into the containers. One after the other after the other, after the other, after the other. We would sing to pass the time, but it was pretty boring and dreadful.

The worst assignment for me was box line. This was where we had to fill cardboard boxes with the bottles of shampoo or shaving cream that were completed and off the line. Generally there were eight to twelve bottles that perfectly fit in each cardboard box. This position was at the end of the line and the speed of the bottles coming off the conveyor belt was insane. I literally had ten seconds to fill an entire box. At the end of the day my hands would be bloody, my fingernails half torn off and multiple blisters on each finger.

After these work experiences, I was determined to finish college and find a better job. Even though these were quirky jobs, I gained a slew of respect for folks that have the stamina to work at these places for years on end.

I Love Pizza, Yes I Do!

One day I found out that my favorite preacher, Joyce Meyer, was going to be holding a conference in Hershey, PA, which is about six hours from our home. I read on the website that it was best to arrive two hours before each session commenced in order to get the best seat. So I brought a good book and waited in anticipation. There were plenty of concession stands selling food and drinks and a book/CD table selling her teachings. I bought a few books and chicken nuggets and settled myself into a great seat. It was perfect for me-- immediately to the right of the stage and on the aisle.

As I was patiently waiting and watching folks being ushered to their seats, several volunteers sang happy birthday to people on the floor seats. I joined in and clapped to at least six happy birthday chants. It was fun, passed the time and kept me occupied. A few minutes after the happy birthdays stopped, the opposite side of the arena began singing "I love pizza. Yes I do!" They were singing with such conviction! All of a sudden people on our side sang back, "I love pizza. Yes I do!" I was clapping and singing and smiling and having a good ole time serenading with all of these strangers. More and more people were shouting at how much they loved the pizza. I popped an average-tasting chicken nugget in my mouth and vowed I was going to try the pizza the next night. If everyone is singing about it, it must be phenomenal! So after the 15th time we sang the I loved pizza song, I glanced over at the woman sitting next to me and she wasn't singing "I love pizza. Yes I do!" at all.

She was singing "I love *Jesus.* Yes I do!'

Did You Eat My Potato?

As part of my loving me treats, I decided to gift myself with a cleaning lady. I work hard and am fortunate enough to be able to hire someone every other week. My friend suggested Sandy, who, in her late fifties, was quite a pistol with the energy of a seven-year-old. Our first meeting went well. She seemed trustworthy and hardworking. As we went over the particulars, she asked me to buy a certain brand of paper towels and a special type of bathroom cleanser. No problem. She lived about twenty minutes from us and was going to charge me five dollars more than other clients because I lived further away. No problem. She also asked if she could eat something in our refrigerator for lunch. No problem-- I *guess*.

Sandy arrived as scheduled on Monday while I was at work. When I walked through the front door that first day, I was in heaven. My feet didn't stick to the floor, the fur balls were gone, the tub sparkled, the toilets were blue, the kitchen smelled like lilacs, the spaghetti sauce splashes had been removed from inside the microwave, the cracker crumbs on the couch disappeared and the air smelled lemony fresh. Ahhhhh! I sat quietly in the living room and savored the clean.

As I glanced around the room, I noticed that a few items on the coffee table had not been there when I left the house that morning. Those items had actually been on the desk in our computer room. I got up and walked around a bit. An angel statue that had been on the shelf in the kitchen was now on an end table in the living room. I noticed several other things but thought to myself they actually looked nice where she put them. I was so grateful the house looked and smelled terrific!

Later that evening my husband, John, asked if I had seen his slippers.

"Nope haven't seen them, check the front hall closet," I replied (knowing him, they were probably on his feet...)

A few minutes later, he stood in front of me like a five-year-old. "I can't find them."

"Did you move things around when you were looking for them? I know how you look for things." If not in plain view, he gives up and beckons me so I can find them.

"Yes hon, I moved things around and they're not there." He hung his head low.

"Maybe they are upstairs in the bedroom closet." I followed him upstairs to our room, now fully engaged in the hunt for the missing slippers.

As I was on my hands and knees searching in our bedroom closet, Becca yelled up from the kitchen. "Mom, did you eat that piece of sausage and pepper pizza in the fridge? I wanted it for dinner!"

"I didn't eat it, maybe it was John."

"It wasn't me. Do you see my slippers?" he questioned.

I was sure they'd be in the closet but no luck. I started to blame menopause for my lack of memory. Becca headed toward her room across the hall.

"Mom, did you take my blue English notebook? It was on my bed when I left for school this morning."

"No honey. I didn't take your blue notebook. Have you seen John's slippers? Did you put them on when you got the mail earlier?"

"Nope. Did you eat my pizza?" She questioned again.

As we were looking for the slippers, notebook and pizza, I noticed that my hair products were on my dresser. This morning they were in the downstairs bathroom. The candles that were on my nightstand were gone. My sneakers, which were generally left outside my closet door, vanished. Becca's winter boots and gloves disappeared also.

Sandy.

I did not want to call her at night but we searched every nook and cranny for the missing items. I called and politely asked Sandy where the missing items were. She told me that she moved the slippers, sneakers, boots and gloves into a large plastic bin in the basement. The side of the basement where we keep our Christmas decorations and lawn furniture. The side of the basement that we visit only twice a year. The pizza was in her belly. The notebook was in one of my daughter's dresser drawers.

Sandy didn't last too long with us.

Before she started with us I had referred her to a friend. On her first day there Sandy ate the only item in her fridge-- a lone baked potato.

Special Feet

We are given what we are given at birth. I have fortunately (or unfortunately) inherited the length of my father's nose and the ball at the end of my mother's nose. Instead of one or the other I was blessed with both. Over time I have overcome and accepted my length and ball. They are a part of me and I have embraced them.

Apparently, I have also been gifted with special attention-getting feet. For some reason people have a special fondness for my feet. I look at them and they look like average feet to me. My pinky toe is little and the increase in toe length is proportional all the way up to my big toe. I like to keep my nails trim and neat. I do have dry spots on the bottom of my heels but try to use lotion to make them smooth. My big toe looks like a Fred Flintstone toe after Fred dropped a rock on it and it's big and pulsating. It is a bit oversized (not freakishly oversized) but has a nice round plumpness to it. It meshes nicely with the other toes but really is not exceptional.

When I was a freshman in college I went to a party at my roommate's house. There were tons of students there, including Grant, a senior friend of my roommate's boyfriend. I was sitting in the living room couch wearing jeans and high heeled sandals. Grant opened his first beer, sat next to me and told me that he liked my feet. I glanced down at my well groomed pink polished toes and giggled. As the night moved on, he followed me from room to room and started hitting on me. I was not into him but was pleasant and made small talk. It was getting late and I was exhausted so I quietly slipped upstairs into my friend's bedroom, pulled out my sleeping bag, found a spot between the twin beds and crashed. About 20 minutes after I settled in, I heard rustling in the room. I was almost asleep and thought it was my girlfriend. Then I heard the zipper of my sleeping bag slowly being unzipped, tooth by tooth. My eyes popped open as I felt a large body squeeze into the bag with me. His leg nuzzled into the sleeping bag and I felt razor stubble on my cheek.

"WHAT ARE YOU DOING?" I exclaimed.

He told me I had the sexiest feet he had ever seen and he wanted to be with me. No way. I recall yelling at him to get out of my sleeping bag and leave me alone. I think the term weirdo might have slipped out of my mouth. He got up and angrily stomped off.

A few years later I was in this posh restaurant in Newburyport with some friends. I went to the ladies room and was about fifth in line. I had on a nice pair of black high heeled sandals and a short denim skirt. I was waiting in line and the woman in front of me smiled.

She looked down and said, "Can I tell you that you have beautiful feet? I really like your toes."

"Seriously?" I thought as I glanced down.

I looked amused and said thanks. She kept on staring down and I began to feel uncomfortable, as if I forgot to put pants on or something. Luckily a stall opened up! Unfortunately the door did not reach the floor so I can only imagine where her eyes went as I shut the door. I looked down again-- big, fat ordinary toes. This toe thing will forever be a mystery to me.

Laughter - The Most Cost Effective Way To Increase Your Joy

- My friend was playing with his two-year-old daughter. She was on his lap, upside down giggling. She looked up at her father's face and said, "Daddy, why do you have grass growing in your nose?"

- My cat Dexter loves to be hugged and held. When working at home my computer is set up on the kitchen table and he jumps up on the table wanting to be held. One time he was squirming as I tried to pick him up and my finger went straight up his butt. Afterwards, when he saw me, his eyes would bulge and he would run out of the room.

- When Becca was 11, I was waiting to drive her to her friend's house. I looked over at the passenger seat and became aggravated because she spilled her cherry juice box on the tan plush seat. When she got in the car I asked her when she spilled the drink on the seat. She innocently looked at me and said "That's not a juice box stain mom, it's my period."

- During the height of Toy Story popularity I wanted to buy my daughter the Buzz Lightyear and Woody dolls. I went to several toy stores. They all stocked plenty of Buzz's but for the life of me I could not find a Woody. One day after going to at least ten stores, I innocently walked up to a young nineteen-year-old employee and asked him, "Do you have a Woody?" When I saw his eyes bulge I realized what I had said. Oh my.

- My good friend was living in an apartment that was attached to her landlord's house. Her landlords were an elderly couple. Her apartment had a kitchen and living room downstairs and her bedroom shared a wall with her landlord's bedroom on the top floor. Her landlord would come over and fix things for her while she was at work. It was a very trusting and amicable relationship. One day she and her boyfriend came home after work and when she went upstairs to get changed, she noticed two sponges attached to her bed posts against the wall.

- When I first started dating John, I went over my dear friend's house to introduce him to her and her Irish husband, Liam. Liam asked John how old he was. John replied "I'm 43." Liam responded in his Irish accent, "You're farty tree?"

- Becca, 10, and I went to my sister's for a home demonstration party. Becca wanted something to drink and whispered if she could have some SCHWEE-PEAS. "What?" She pointed to bottle of Schweppes ginger ale.

- One of my first professional jobs was at a law firm. I worked with another young woman in the basement. It was a casual environment and we always had the radio on. One day I was singing along with the song on the radio, "Immaculate conception, going to tell all the world that I love you" and Sharon asked me what the heck I was singing. She cracked up and pointed out that the words were "In my midnight confession".

- While John and I were in Sedona Arizona, we splurged on a helicopter ride through the red rocks. As we were waiting in the lobby, I admitted that I was pretty nervous about the flight. We had just been told that the helicopter did not have any doors. We would be secured only with a lap seatbelt. John said he wasn't nervous at all. My husband is a quiet man who loves adventure, but does not enjoy socializing in big crowds. He replied with a classic line. "Hon, you being nervous about going on the helicopter is like me being nervous about going to a party."

- I mentioned to John's step-mother that I took my stepson to a tapas place for his 18th birthday. Her face dropped. "You took him to a topless place?"

- One hot summer day, I went shopping with Becca, my friend, and her 3 beautiful girls (all of Irish descent). I bought each of us a chocolate bar and within minutes most of the chocolate had melted. Everyone had to scoop the soft liquid chocolate off the paper and lick our fingers. I told my friend she had a chocolate spot on her cheek. She tried to wipe it off with a napkin. It was still there. She dabbed the napkin with water and wiped her face again and it was still there. We moved on to another topic. She texted me later and said "Remember that chocolate that was on my face? It was a clump of freckles."

- During game night, Becca's seventeen-year-old male friends were posed the question, "What is the most common bra size?" The boys deliberated and answered 18-I.

- A coworker of mine asked me if I knew Nutella. It was new to the market and he loved it! I responded, "No, does she work in the call center?"

- When I was fifteen I had a mad crush on my neighbor's nephew. He was a few years older than me and was visiting from New York. He was so cute, hot, nice teeth, and a total dude. I was next door talking to him, his aunt and an older female relative. The four of us had a nice conversation and all of a sudden my relative, who shall remain unnamed, went ppppffffftttt!. Oh my-- an air biscuit! I know it just slipped out, but did it have to be at that moment?

- I had been very open with Becca and talked to her beforehand about menstruation. She knew exactly what to expect. When she "became a woman" she crabbed, complained and was completely miserable to be around. She came to me on the fifth day and said, "Thank God that's over!" She thought that was it... forever.

- I was walking down the street near my work and walking towards me was Buddy Hackett. I said, "Buddy Hackett?" He replied "Yesh?"

- When my daughter was a toddler, we moved into a brand new neighborhood. Our neighbors were building their house and asked if they could use our water spigot until they got their spigot hooked up. Absolutely. They told us that friends of theirs would be helping and it was fine by me that they use our water. One morning I got up early because Becca wanted a drink. I generally wear just a t-shirt to bed. I dropped her bottle and bent down to pick it up-- knowing full well I was commando, but it was 5:30 AM. I turned and looked out my slider and there were three firemen out by my water spigot in view of the full moon.

- During my mother's funeral dinner, my friends and I were sitting at a table together. I began to talk to a friend who's dad passed away right before my mother. It was a solemn moment. I turned to my other friend Kellie and she had two pieces of long chicklet gum protruding out of her mouth like Bugs Bunny. Guess no solemn talk for us!

- I was having dinner with a dear friend at an Italian restaurant. As she was telling a story in the middle of dinner, I watched a healthy, bite-sized piece of eggplant parmesan leave her mouth, fly through the air and land on my cheek. Plop.

The Older I Get

The older I get the ***more*** I:

- Realize that family is a true gift in life.

- Know there are many different ways to show love.

- Understand that beauty is truly inside a person's heart.

- Tend to forgive more quickly.

- Don't sweat the small stuff.

- Appreciate snuggling with my kitties.

- Value my friends and feel a certain 'oneness' with them.

- Believe in miracles.

- Appreciate brutal honesty from others.

- Move aside when an aggressive driver is behind me.

- Want to go out there and accomplish my dreams.

- Believe that those little things in life mean the most.

- Realize I cannot please everyone... and that's okay.

- Want to help those who are in pain.

- Try to break through my limiting beliefs.

- Appreciate the small, seemingly insignificant, things in life.

- Enjoy nature and its beauty.

- Floss

- Have to remove unwanted stray hairs.

- See the good in others.

- Reach out for help when I'm troubled.

- Accept that bad things just happen.

- Understand that when I'm in a tough situation, it might be an opportunity for me to learn and grow.

- Get that people all over the world want to be loved, just like I do.

- Realize how fortunate I am.

- Understand that my body is just a vessel and will eventually break down.

- Believe my spirit will live on when I pass away.

- Want to do things to please myself.

- Am able to laugh at myself.

- Cannot remember where I put things.

- Am inspired and driven to pursue my dreams.

- Understand that if my dreams don't come true, I can pat myself on the back for trying my best.

- My best is good enough.

- Accept myself the way I am...flaws and all.

- Realize that I can't judge someone until I've walked in the same shoes.

- Sense that people really do come in our lives for a reason.

- Treasure the wisdom of the elderly.

- Take responsibility for my actions.

- Am aware of my limitations.

- Eat fruits and vegetables.

- Value time with friends.

- Know my parents love me and did the best they could.

- Appreciate the sacrifices my family made for me.

- Love to melt into a good bear hug.

- Have room in my heart for unconditional love.

- Try to understand other people's viewpoints.

- Know that God loves me.

- Trust myself and my inner guidance.

- Can sit still in silence.

- Want to just go for it!

- Know that a compliment can make someone's day.

- Realize that really listening to someone takes action.

- Am open to different types of religious beliefs.

The older I get the **_less_** I:

- Yearn for material things.

- Want to impress others.

- Hold onto negative thoughts.

- Yearn to be in the "popular" crowd.

- Care that I change into my jammies at 5:30 PM.

- Want clutter in my house.

- Act like a raving lunatic when things don't go my way.

- Stress about climbing the career ladder.

- Get upset about small stuff.

- Engage in malicious gossip.

- Want to argue with someone who has a different idea than me.

- Tolerate those who think they are better than someone else.

- Menstruate.

- Rely on others to make me happy.

- Want to focus only on my problems.

- Am brutal on myself when I make a mistake.

- Get nervous when trying something new (as long as it won't kill me).

- Berate myself.

- Feel the need to be rushing around all the time.

- Care about what others think of me.

- Judge others for being different.

- Tolerate bullying.

- Care that I put my candies in a Waterford bowl.

- Keep quiet on an issue that is important to me.

- Hold back from taking a risk.